THIS IS **SINGAPORE**

First published in 2017

Talisman Publishing Pte Ltd
talisman@apdsing.com
www.talismanpublishing.com
ISBN 978-981-11-2389-4

Printed in Malaysia

PAGE 1 A vertical garden in the Central
Business District celebrating Singapore's 50
years of independence, known locally as SG50.
OPPOSITE One of the commemorative designs
for SG50, a collaboration between Singaporean
firm, Supermama, and Japanese porcelain
company Kihara Inc. The plate features 50
Singapore icons, with first prime minister Lee
Kuan Yew famously shedding tears at the centre.
OVERLEAF Clockwise from top left: Super-
modern entrance to the National Gallery
Singapore; signage at the ArtScience Museum
at Marina Bay; Wavy reflective cladding at ION,
a mall on Orchard Road; gleaming commercial
towers in the Central Business District; steps to
the Louis Vuitton store at Marina Bay; high-rise
greenery at the PARKROYAL on Pickering hotel.
PAGES 6–7 Evening view from the roof of the
Esplanade theatre complex over the Padang to
the former Supreme Court building.

THIS IS SINGAPORE

BY KIM INGLIS
PHOTOGRAPHY BY JACOB TERMANSEN

TALISMAN

CONTENTS

THE MAKING OF A MODERN NATION

"Singapore must retain the sense of space. We're going to build taller buildings but we can't build them closely together. There must be a sense of playing fields, and recreational areas for children and old people — a sense that this is a full country with all the facilities which you expect of a large country but in a confined space."

— Lee Kuan Yew, 2005

Today, the city-state of Singapore is much loved by its residents and much admired around the world. With a maritime history spanning over 700 years, it reached a milestone in 2015 when the country celebrated 50 years as an independent nation.

Singapore's story has always incorporated change: in the 14th century it was home to the Malay kingdom of Temasek; in the 19th and first half of the 20th century it was a British trading post; and after World War II it gained its independence. Despite sketchy records, it is now established that Temasek was a cosmopolitan trading post that made full use of its strategically located harbour, as did the British when they established Singapore as a free port in 1819. Today, trade is still important, but in recent decades the country has reinvented itself, diversified and expanded massively, looking to both Asia and the international stage for relevance.

Singapore is economically successful, has high literacy rates and a healthcare and pension scheme that is extremely robust. Singaporeans are, for the most part, hardworking and dedicated; they are rightfully proud of their forward-looking, modern nation and should be congratulated on being a peaceful, multi-ethnic and multi-religious country in a world that is anything but.

In this book, we try to present Singapore as it is today. We look at its culture, its people, its topography and its heritage. We show through eye-catching photography its quirks and its character. But what we see on the surface and what exists in actuality are not always the same. That is true for most nations.

This first chapter looks at the downtown core. Outwardly, the look is very 21st century: There's a mix of newly constructed and historical buildings scattered around a relatively small landmass and a truly spectacular city centre around Marina Bay. An efficient network of roads and railways connects this central core with a number of satellite residential areas, while swathes of tropical jungle spread out across the central catchment area. Inwardly, the country can probably best be described as conservative with a small "c"; for sure, there are risk-takers, but for the most part the population is content to be led forward responsibly rather than recklessly.

Taking the best of the best from around the world and matching these with quixotic home-grown elements has resulted in a unique mix: unlike many countries, Singapore doesn't try to hide its colonial past. Rather, it celebrates its heritage, updates it where necessary, and constantly keeps its eye on the future.

Much has been made of Singapore's meteoric rise from third-world to first-world status since colonial rule ended in 1959. Some of it is true, but a lot is exaggerated. As the country forges forward, it is a good moment to examine how it emerged from a largely suburban land of *kampungs* and *kopitiams* to become one of the region's leading economies. One well-known commentator who should know better has even talked of how Singapore went, virtually overnight, from "swamp to skyscrapers".

As with most tall tales, the truth is considerably less dramatic. By the time Singapore exited from its merger with the Federation of Malaya in 1963 and gained eventual independence two years later, it already had a thriving economic and cultural life. Certainly, work was needed in terms of social development, but it was hardly the poverty-stricken backwater some pundits claim.

There were few resources, and much investment was needed — and obtained. On the residential front, high-rises flats were established outside the city centre, and a massive land reclamation project in the 1970s and 1980s alleviated the constraints of space. The government realized that it could not rely solely on trade for survival, and it expanded into other areas, such as finance, manufacturing and oil refining.

Indeed, as the government spearheaded growth and higher standards of living, it still maintains a strong link with Singapore's past history.

PREVIOUS PAGE The ArtScience Museum, built in the shape of a lotus, has changing exhibitions that fuse art and science to tell fascinating stories.
ABOVE Singapore's city centre is characterised by its fusion of colonial-era edifices and cutting-edge modern architecture.
OPPOSITE Old combines with new in a mixed-use development. The central building, flanked by hotel towers, is the old drill hall of the Straits Settlements Volunteer Force (1907).

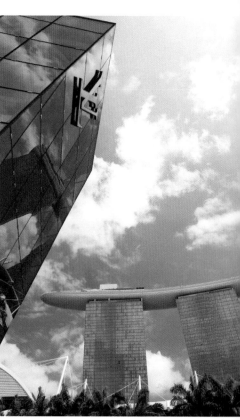

This delicate balancing act between the past and the present is fully realized in Singapore's Marina Bay metropolitan core. Conceptualised from at least the 1970s when the authorities realized that the financial centre needed land for expansion, the development seamlessly extends Singapore's downtown district — so much so that most people have forgotten what was there before: the sea. Situated at the mouth of the historic Singapore River, it incorporates many heritage buildings around the Padang and Esplanade with a slew of glass-and-concrete skyscrapers. The Marina barrage, a dam built across the Marina Channel, facilitates the creation of the island's 15th reservoir, while around its rim runs a 3.5km boardwalk promenade. It's a good place to hop onto a river taxi or simply stroll around on a sunny day.

Attractions, beside the verdant Gardens by the Bay, include the bug-eyed Esplanade concert hall and theatre complex, the Marina Bay Sands integrated resort and casino, numerous shopping and f&b outlets, a floating performance platform, and the cutting-edge ArtScience Museum in the shape of a gigantic lotus. Nearby are a statue of Singapore's merlion symbol at the mouth of the Singapore river; the ingeniously curved and latticed metal pedestrian bridge shaped on the design of a double helix; the Singapore Flyer ferris wheel; and a number of world-class hotels.

Dominating all, however, is the triple-tower Marina Bay Sands complex — or MBS as it is commonly known in the land of the acronym. Opened in 2010, it was designed by Moshe Safdie and Associates and comprises three elegantly curved 60-storey towers topped by a ship-like structure known as the Skypark. In the words of its architect: 'Marina Bay Sands is really more than a building project, it is a microcosm of a city rooted in Singapore's culture, climate and contemporary life.'

OPPOSITE TOP Various views of the Marina Bay Sands, double helix bridge and Singapore Flyer. OPPOSITE BELOW Designed by leading local firm DP Architects, the Esplanade performing arts complex features two eye-catching spiky domes. LEFT The vision of the late Lee Kuan Yew, Singapore's first Prime Minister, the Marina Barrage dams the mouth of the Marina Channel to create the city-state's 15th reservoir — and the first in the heart of the city.

The elements of Singapore's red-and-white national flag represent a nation on the ascendant: red stands for equality, white symbolises virtue, the crescent moon represents the young nation and the five stars depict democracy, peace, progress, justice and equality.

ABOVE Built in 1999 to a design by the Public Works Department, the Parliament building was designed to represent a contemporary architectural expression of stateliness and authority. OPPOSITE Clockwise from top left: Skyscrapers in the extended Central Business District adjacent Marina Bay; CBD offices with a close-up of One Fullerton; modern piazza before the Capitol Theatre; Norman Foster's Supreme Court building as viewed from the National Gallery rooftop.

In addition to these gleaming behemoths of modernity, a slew of heritage structures coexist with their new neighbours while demonstrating an earlier story. This comes in the form of Sir Stamford Raffles arriving at the mouth of the Singapore River on 28 January 1819, surveying the naturally deep harbour and abundant fresh water supplies and on the spot establishing Singapore as a free port. He shrewdly assessed the island's potential as a base for England's merchant fleet to forestall advances by the Dutch, England's great rival in the region, and acted with alacrity.

This is a tale oft told. What may not be so well known is how much planning went into the layout of the fledgling trading hub. Raffles realized that the river would be the nexus from which the new colony would thrive — but where to build around it was not so clearcut. The land on the river's north bank was level and firm, but the southern bank was swampy. Nonetheless, as Singapore was to 'become a place of considerable magnitude and importance', Raffles deemed that 'an economical and proper allotment of the ground intended to form the site of the principal town is an object of first importance'.

Building on the experience of the East India Company in the colonization of Indian cities, where a fort often dominated the town and various areas — residential, governmental,

military and mercantile — were kept separate from the local populace, was a start. In such towns as Calcutta, grand civic buildings signifying the might of Empire were laid out between swathes of green denoting prosperity and good sanitation. The town plan of George Town in Penang, with its grid of well-ordered streets and separate areas for Chinese, Indians and Malays, was also consulted.

Raffles set up a Town Planning Committee under one military man, Captain David, one civil servant, George Bonham and one merchant, A L Johnson. He also enlisted the help of surveyor Lieutenant Philip Jackson to draw up the earliest known map of Singapore. The resulting Town Plan focused on the area that now comprises downtown Singapore: stretching from Telok Ayer Bay in the west across the Singapore river and east to the Kallang River, much of the early settlement remains intact today. It was a well laid-out town that comprised some key areas (see overleaf).

OPPOSITE Clockwise from top left: The last building to be constructed in neo-Classical style, the former Supreme Court building (1937–39) is now part of the National Gallery; this distinctive red-and-white brick edifice (1909) is the oldest fire station and also houses a heritage gallery; classical colonnade at the former convent of CHIJMES; elephant statue outside the former Parliament building (1827).

GOVERNMENT AREA: The area between Fort Canning and the Singapore River was set aside for a cantonment with military and civic buildings. Centred around the Padang, many civic buildings have now been converted into galleries, museums and the like. This building houses the Asian Civilisations Museum (ACM).

FORT CANNING: This fortified hillock, built on the ancient fortifications of Temasek, formed the northernmost boundary of the early settlement. It still looks down over the colonial core, and has lovely parkland as well as some original colonial buildings. There is also a reminder of the colony's first cemetery (above).

SINGAPORE RIVER: Land lining the Singapore River was reserved for commercial and mercantile purposes — office buildings, godowns and the like. These still remain in the same area: the old warehouses, merchants' offices and shophouses have been revitalised as food and beverage venues at Clarke and Boat Quay, while Commercial Square is now bristling with skyscrapers in the Central Business District. This photo shows the Anderson Bridge (1910) and the Fullerton Hotel behind.

The progress of my new settlement is in every way most satisfactory, and it would gladden your heart to witness the activity and cheerfulness that prevail throughout; every day brings us new settlers, and Singapore has already become a great emporium.

— Stamford Raffles, letter, 12 January 1823

CHINATOWN: The area in the southwest and in the existing Chinese *kampong* was reserved for the Chinese settlement. This still exists today as a somewhat sanitised Chinatown, stretching from Tanjong Pagar to the river. This streamlined Moderne shophouse building at the junction of Keong Saik and Teck Lim roads was designed by self-taught architect Kwan Yow Luen in 1938.

KAMPONG GLAM: The area around the residence of the Sultan known as Kampong Glam was reserved for Malays, Bugis settlers and Arab merchants. It still exists today as a 'Malay area', but later gentrification has resulted in a quirky mix of old and new. This photo depicts the Sultan Mosque, the second mosque to be built on the site; it was designed by Denis Santry of Swan & Maclaren in Indo-Saracenic style.

INDIAN ENCLAVE: An area further north of the fledgling settlement was discussed and tentatively reserved for Indian merchants, financiers and the like. It now exists as 'Little India', a vibrant mini sub-continental town. Here we see a stall-holder selling an assortment of paraphernalia, ranging from flower garlands to *paan*, vegetables and spices.

> *From the Singapore River to Marina Bay, we've totally transformed Singapore over the last half century. 1959 was a moment of great change, but nobody at the Padang in June 1959 imagined the change to today's Singapore. It was not possible. We will continue to improve our lives provided we work together and remain a harmonious and a cohesive society — so that in another 50 years we will have built another Singapore which is equally unimaginable today. The key is to stay united through rain or shine.*

— Prime Minister Lee Hsien Loong, 16 August 2009

In addition, the Raffles Town Plan stipulated that there be a market at Telok Ayer, a church and clear demarcation between races and professions. Even today, much of this early zoning still remains in the grid-like pattern of streets and the ethnic enclaves (although ethnical segregation obviously no longer exists) and many landmarks remain.

Opposite, clockwise from top left, we see two views of Singapore's original Esplanade, sited on the left bank of the Singapore River. Planted with shade-bearing trees such as angsana and rain trees, it bordered the Padang and was a popular place for an evening stroll in colonial times. Although no longer on the water's front, it is still a leafy enclave, with remnants of an earlier era: a Victorian fountain and a memorial to war hero Lim Bo Seng are seen here.

27 June 1887 was Jubilee Day commemorating the 50th anniversary of Queen Victoria's reign; it was celebrated in style the length and breadth of the British Empire. In Singapore, a statue of Sir Stamford Raffles costing $20,446.10 was installed in the middle of the Padang. In 1919, 100 years after Raffles founded the settlement, the statue was moved to its present site in front of the Town Hall.

The site selected by Raffles for the first Anglican church, also designed by Coleman, today houses a second church — St Andrew's Cathedral (1856). The original church was twice hit by lightning and deemed unsafe, so was demolished and replaced with this elegant building with its imposing spire. Built from brick, with a roof of slate and teak, it is covered with fine *chunam* plaster: favoured by colonial designers for its insect resistance and brilliant white colour, the plaster is made from a mix of shell, lime, egg white, coarse sugar and water in which coconut husks have been steeped.

The *grande dame* of markets in Singapore is Lau Pa Sat or Telok Ayer Market. Originally designed by George Coleman, the architect of many early colonial buildings, it was moved from its original waterfront location and rebuilt in 1894 to specifications by municipal engineer James MacRitchie. Even though it has since undergone more than a couple of restorations and additions, it still combines history, local food and atmosphere beneath an elegant cast-iron structure with intricate filigree work.

Taken from the Malay word for 'field' or 'plain', the Padang has been the venue for many a momentous event in Singapore. During the early days it was surrounded by both civic buildings and residences of early colonial pioneers — and was the place to see and be seen. In the past and today, it hosts sporting events, celebrations and more. Key events at the Padang include the surrender of Japanese forces on 12 September 1945, the first National Day celebration on 9 August 1966, and the SG50 series of events 50 years later.

All these sites, and more, may be seen on the 'Jubilee Walk', a route around the reclaimed waterfront that was mapped out by various agencies, including the Ministry of Culture, Community and Youth, the National Heritage Board, the National Parks Board, the Urban Redevelopment Authority and National Arts Council. Stretching from Fort Canning to the extended Central Business District, it tells Singapore's story more eloquently than this author's words.

Unlike many ex-colonies, Singapore has never shied away from its colonial past. In fact, it has positively embraced its history. In the same way that Singapore has retained its free port status, its British legal system, even the English language post-Independence, it maintains many of its civic, commercial and cultural buildings from the colonial era — and uses them commercially today.

Over the years, heritage experts and architecture conservationists have bemoaned what they consider the widescale destruction of many of Singapore's neo-Palladian and Renaissance-style edifices. But, if one were to walk around the old downtown colonial core with eyes wide open, it is amazing how many of these Victorian and Edwardian buildings can still be seen, their imposing facades looking over the harbour, river and Padang as if frozen in time.

A closer look, however, reveals that they aren't frozen at all. While the religious and cultural buildings, for the most part, keep to their original usage, many other grandiose edifices in the city centre have been restored, re-designed and re-fitted for a new purpose. Old government offices at Empress Place now house the cutting-edge Asian Civilisations Museum; the adjacent

old Parliament is today an arts centre. Across the Padang, the former Supreme Court and City Hall have been transformed into the National Gallery Singapore, while over the river the General Post Office has been reinvented as a five-star hotel.

Up on Fort Canning, old barracks have found new life, while the compound of the Convent of the Holy Infant Jesus dating from 1913 has been converted into a buzzing food and beverage centre. Just down the road, the famous Capitol Theatre and Building, built in the 1930s, retains only its old façade. Somewhat controversially, it was remodelled into a multi-functional entertainment space with offices, residences, a new theatre, plenty of shops and restaurants, as well as a courtyard piazza.

OPPOSITE Clockwise from top left: Gothic-style gate at Fort Canning Green, site of the first Christian graveyard. The letters are *iota*, *eta* and *sigma*, the first three letters of the Greek word for Jesus. Part of the facade of the Capitol building (1933), designed by the architectural firm Keys & Dowdeswell. The building contained one of Singapore's only air-conditioned cinemas. View of the fine 'streaky bacon' brick detailing on the Hill Street Fire Station. Detail of the Arts House (former Parliament building).

THE
GARDEN
CITY

Given our land constraints, we have sought practical and innovative solutions to integrate greenery and biodiversity into our urban environment, through our parks, park connectors, streetside planting, water networks and sky-rise greenery. In this way, we also improve the quality of our living environment.

— Urban Redevelopment Authority, 2014

When a large monitor lizard decided to stroll across the track at the 2016 Singapore Grand Prix, visitors to Singapore exclaimed at the sight of a huge reptile in such a densely populated part of the city. Yet, for those who live in Singapore, it wasn't such a surprise. They know the island is home to a large range of both aquatic and terrestrial wildlife such as otters, pythons, monkeys, monitor lizards and endangered pangolins as well as 450 species of birds. In fact, a family of rare otters has taken up residence in the waters of Gardens by the Bay in the city centre.

According to a 2011 study by researchers at the National University of Singapore, 56 percent of the island is covered in vegetation, with 29 percent consisting of spontaneous green areas and 27 percent consisting of managed green areas like parks and golf courses.

Given the city-state's small land area and the need for economic growth, the government constantly has to balance development with biodiversity conservation. There are invariably mistakes, such as the decision to ultimately build over the Bukit Brown cemetery, an area of both historical and ecological importance, but there are success stories

too. These include the regeneration of mangroves at the Sungeh Buloh Wetland Reserve and a similar project on the rustic island of Pulau Ubin. There is also the case of Singapore's Botanic Gardens receiving UNESCO World Heritage status.

In addition to large areas of green, many of which are also used for recreational purposes, urban planting is also taken seriously. Highways, overhead walkways and streets are always beautifully lined with trees, bougainvillea and tropical ornamentals, and in recent years sky-rise greenery has started to add a new dimension to the city's greening. While rooftop and vertical greenery is not a new architectural phenomenon in Singapore, conservationists argue that 'unmanaged greenery', such as that at Bukit Brown, should be given as high a priority as 'managed greenery'. How this story unfolds is one to watch.

PREVIOUS PAGE The hotel PARKROYAL on Pickering, designed by Singapore-based WOHA Architects, is a showcase for high-rise greenery.

OPPOSITE A tranquil beach on Sentosa, protected by the Sentosa Development Corporation, set up in 1972 to balance sustainability with leisure development.

> *If a garden is well maintained and neatly landscaped, there must be a dedicated and efficient gardener.*
>
> — Lee Kuan Yew, 1959

ABOVE An area of the Chinese themed garden at Gardens by the Bay with MBS in the background. OPPOSITE TOP The Gardens' Supertree Grove was designed by a British landscaping firm, and contains more than 200 species and varieties of bromeliads, orchids, ferns and tropical flowering climbers on the 18 'trees'. OPPOSITE BELOW The Symphony Stage on a lake in Palm Valley at the Botanic Gardens is a popular venue for concerts.

Equatorial Singapore has always been very green. Hot and humid year round, it used to be covered in dense tropical rainforest with swamps inland and mangroves on the coast. Today, somewhat surprisingly for such an urban environment, about half of its 700 square kilometres of land is green. Although much of this comprises military training grounds, there are also parks, reservoirs, farms and nature reserves.

Visitors note that the country has enviable eco credentials with sound water conservation policies, a strong environmental ethos and a fervent promotion of green recreation. In colonial times the first forest reserves were set up, then, at the time of Independence, the first prime minister Lee Kuan Yew embarked on an ambitious project to create a city-state within a garden environment. His famous tree-planting forays under the umbrella of the so-called Parks and Trees Unit eventually morphed into today's massive National Parks Board.

Today, NParks (as it is affectionately known) is entrusted with the maintenance and promotion of Singapore's green spaces — from its four nature reserves and over 300 parks, to park connectors, lush street plantings, green recreation areas and more. It says its mission is 'to create the best living environment through excellent greenery and recreation in partnership with the community'. This is a huge undertaking as the government has set aside nine percent of the island for parks and nature reserves, and has promised that 85 percent of Singaporeans will live within 400 metres of parkland by 2030. This is a not inconsiderable amount for a country that is the second most densely populated in the world (Monaco is the first).

> *This island should all be cleared and cultivated; in fact become a large Garden.*
>
> — Goal of the Agricultural and Horticultural Society,
> *Singapore Free Press*, 6 April 1837

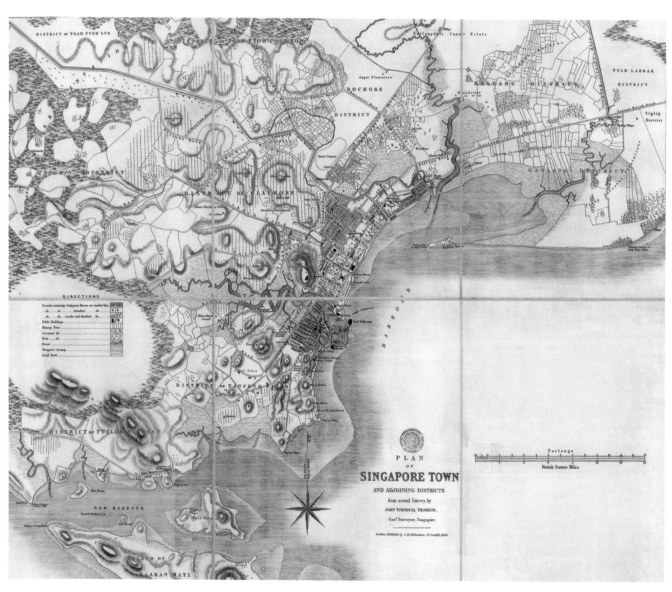

ABOVE A wonderfully detailed map from 1846 of 'Singapore Town and Adjoining Districts', from a survey by John Turnbull Thomson, clearly outlines the pepper, gambier and coconut plantations north and west of the main city.

OPPOSITE LEFT A small Spice Garden, a replica of Raffles' experimental garden on Fort Canning Hill, contains a number of important spices and herbs.
OPPOSITE RIGHT Nutmeg, cloves and cinnamon — all early crops.

Early Plantations

Even though trade was the primary motivation for the founding of Singapore, botany was also high on the agenda. From the earliest days, Raffles had established a small experimental garden on Fort Canning Hill, employing the botanist Nathanial Wallich to supervise progress. Wallich noted that the soil and climate of Singapore was most prescient for extensive cultivation, and by 1836 an Agricultural and Horticultural Society had been founded with the goal of promoting 'the improvement of every branch of Agriculture in the Settlement'.

Pre 1819, gambier plantations were already in existence in the island's interior. Run by Chinese and Malays, the gambier was mainly exported to China. The British proceeded to encourage other forms of agriculture, and from the 1820s onwards, a variety of different plantations sprung up to the north and west of the settlement. These early plantations concentrated on gambier and pepper, two crops that tend to grow entwined around each other in a symbiotic relationship. But Raffles was keen to break the Dutch monopoly on the Spice

Trade and supply 'all the spices needed by the civilized worl'. As his nutmeg seeds and plants from Bencoolen flourished on Fort Canning Hill, British planters became keen to get in on the act.

Clearing land in the Tanglin and Claymore areas, their nutmeg plantations thrived here in the 1830s and 1940s. Typically, the topography featured groves of nutmeg trees surrounding hilltop bungalows named after their owners — Oxley, Carnie, Prinsep, Cuppage, Scott, and the like. Initially successful, nutmeg production later became compromised by a disease, so other crops such as cocoa, coffee, cinnamon, cloves and sugar cane were introduced and coconuts were planted in coastal areas. However, in the late 1850s, this 'nutmeg canker' spread across the island and spread to every plantation, and by 1862 nutmeg cultivation ceased altogether. The huge estates were divided up and sold, mainly for housing needs.

It would be another 50 years before another crop would replace nutmeg. Spurred on by the invention of the motorcar and the need for tyres, it came in the form of the para rubber tree *(Hevea brasiliensis)*.

"Today, the Black-and-White house is synonymous with the idea of an Englishman's home in Singapore during the colonial era. Their importance, however, extends beyond the merely historical — they are actually damn good houses to live in."

— Julian Davison, 2006
Black and White, The Singapore House 1898–1941

The Black-And-White Estates

Even though the land on which these plantations once stood has now been incorporated into the city, a surprising number of the early estates that replaced the plantations and date from the late 19th century up to the 1930s still exist. Some contained homes for British civil servants, the military and the police, while others were built for private individuals and employees of some of the large companies and banks.

Many such estates contain collections of what are known as Singapore Black-and-White houses — a style of residence that originated with the colonial Public Works Department (PWD) in the 1890s and was developed by architects in private practice in the ensuing decades. Built in expansive parklands, with sweeping lawns, tennis courts and mature trees for shade, such residences represented a lifestyle of ease and elegance that is for the most part lost today.

The architecture of the Black-and-White house is a singular one, not replicated elsewhere. Many have described it as a cross between the vernacular Malay house on stilts and the "Tudorbethan" style, popular at the turn of the century in England, where rendered surfaces were painted white and timber elements were black. Certainly, both influences are apparent, but where the Black-and-White house excels is in its suitability to site

and climate. Being high above ground ensured safety from floods and tropical bugs, snakes and the like; the wooden upper storey absorbed solar radiation less rapidly than a brick house; high ceilings and large rooms at this level encouraged cross ventilation; and capacious verandas and overhanging eaves, along with chick blinds, mitigated heat and glare from the sun.

Even though the basic form remained fairly constant, the style did evolve over time. Early Black-and-Whites took elements from plantation architecture and the Arts and Crafts movement; later ones became more neo-Classical in appearance and proportions, many sporting a *porte-cochère* at the front; while those pre-War lost the stilts and incorporated Modernist and Art Deco aspects.

Regardless, it is to the credit of the government that many of these early estates have been preserved and continue as homes today. A tour or drive around Alexander Park, Ridley Park, Goodwood Hill, Mount Faber or Mount Pleasant is a must-do for heritage aficionados.

OPPOSITE Clockwise from top: The so-called Admiral's House (around 1915) on the elevated promontory of Bukit Chermin, overlooking Labrador Point and Sentosa. One of the 1930s Alexandra Park Black-and-Whites overlooking swathes of lawn. A home in Ridley Park, one of the early inter-war military estates serving the Tanglin Barracks.

> *Connecting people and plants through publications, horticultural and botanical displays, educational outreach and events, provision of a key civic and recreational space, and playing a role as an international garden and a regional centre for botanical and horticultural research and training.*
> — Mission Statement, Singapore Botanic Gardens

Singapore Botanic Gardens

Established in 1859, the Singapore Botanic Gardens has served variously as a recreational pleasure garden, a botanical research facility, a nature conservator and an educator. A colonial institution for much of its history, it lost relevance for a couple of decades after Independence, but bounded back under the Directorship of botanist extraordinaire Dr Tan Wee Kiat (who later went on to establish Gardens by the Bay).

Prior to Singapore's celebration of 50 years of Independence, the government decided to put the Gardens forward for UNESCO World Heritage status. It argued that it is the country's one institution that bridges colonialism and independence; it has acted as a commercial and recreational powerhouse; and its influence has been significant both in Asia and further afield. On 15 May 2015, the bid was accepted, and the Singapore Botanic Gardens became the first and only tropical botanic garden on UNESCO's World Heritage List. It is the first in Asia and the third botanic gardens with this status following Orto Botanico di Padova and the Royal Botanic Gardens, Kew.

Today, the Singapore Botanic Gardens are part botanical institution, part tourist destination and part regional tropical park. Some of the original buildings still exist as does the first lake, Swan Lake, and a four-hectare piece of primaeval forest, the only piece of pristine rain forest left on the island. The National Orchid Garden is a splendid sight, with 60,000 orchid plants representing over 400 species and 2,000 hybrids, and the Herbarium continues as a research centre. All the while, Palm Valley streches down to an extension of the Gardens near Bukit Timah Road.

Culture is a priority these days, also. Concerts, exhibitions and educational displays are ever-changing, whilst a display of garden sculptures adds interest against the backdrop of majestic heritage trees and tropical foliage.

OPPOSITE Paths meander
through dense foliage
and open parkland, whilst
colonial-era remnants such
as this Victorian statue
and the 1860 bandstand
(overleaf) are reminders of
the Gardens' past.

ABOVE TOP The National
Orchid Garden is a riot of
colour and variety.
ABOVE Left to right:
Papaya tree; James Surls'
sculpture inspired by the
seed of the Dipterocarp;
ornamental waterfall.

ABOVE The bandstand
more or less maintains its
original 1860 form. Over
the years it has been used
as a venue for concerts,
games and gatherings.
OPPOSITE Rubber trees
are few and far between
now in Singapore, but these
examples from Pulau Ubin
and the Science Centre
showcase how the trees were
planted in straight lines.
The herringbone method
of tapping was pioneered by
'Mad Ridley' at the Gardens.

One of the Botanic Gardens' great success stories concerns the propagation of the Brazilian native para rubber tree. How it ended up in Singapore and Malaya is a tale that involves elements of entrepreneurship, endurance and plain simple good luck.

In 1876, 70,000 seedlings were sent from Brazil to Kew Gardens where botanists only managed to germinate three percent. Of 22 seedlings sent to Singapore the following year, nine were sent to Kuala Kangsar in Perak, 11 were sown in the Singapore Botanic Gardens, and the remaining two were probably planted in Malacca. Over the next ten years, they did not do well, and it was only when Henry Nicholas Ridley became director of the Botanic Gardens (1888–1912) that progress was made. His dedication, even obsession, with para rubber propagation led to his moniker "Mad Ridley", as he ceaselessly travelled around Singapore and Malaya trying to persuade planters to take on the challenge of rubber planting.

Eventually a world glut of coffee (ironically from Brazil), an increased demand for car and bicycle tyres, and Ridley's new latex tapping method resulted in Malayan planters giving rubber a go. By the outbreak of World War II, 40 percent of Singapore's land mass was planted with rubber and rubber production soared from 400 tons in 1905 to over 210,000 tons in 1920. Rubber is still one of Malaysia's biggest exports today.

Today, in Singapore, some rubber trees still continue to thrive in Palm Valley and near the Herbarium in the Botanic Gardens, as well as in the forests of Seletar and Bukit Timah. Where they are most in evidence, though, is in the abandoned rubber plantations on Pulau Ubin and Pulau Tekong. There, they are still visible in their original plantation form in long lines, but now their serried ranks are gradually being incorporated into the wider landscape of secondary forest coverage.

"I have always believed that a blighted urban landscape, a concrete jungle destroys the human spirit. We need the greenery of nature to lift our spirits."

— Lee Kuan Yew, 1995

Gardens by the Bay

Described by its chief executive, Dr Tan Wee Kiat, as 'Wisley Gardens meets Kew', this groundbreaking public power garden is one of Singapore's latest greening projects. Sandwiched between the Marina Bay barrage and the monumental MBS on what was until recently a toxic wasteland of reclaimed ground, it is an extraordinary example of public greening. Covering 110 acres, it houses more than a million plants and cost more than S$1bn. In an almost alchemical feat, the gardens seemed to sprout almost overnight.

Comprising two superb cooled glass domes, a grove of Supertrees (fantastical structures covered with climbers, bromeliads and flowering plants that open up to the sunlight like inverted umbrellas), a number of themed smaller gardens and plentiful cycling and walking paths, the Gardens by the Bay are a fitting testament to the country's delicate balance between built hardscapes and the desire for trees and plants.

It is a testament to Dr Tan's vision that the two conservatories and the Supertree grove have now been accepted as iconic symbols of Singapore. So indelibly are they now imprinted in the Singapore physical and metaphorical landscape, it's hard to imagine that a few years ago they didn't exist.

LEFT Clockwise from top left: Aerial walkway in the Supertree grove; Crepe Ginger flower (*Costus speciosus*); Pitcher Plant (*Nepenthes* sp) from the Cloud Forest Dome. Dragonfly sculptures by local artist, Dr Elsie Yu; statue of a laughing Buddha by Wang Rong Hai under a Bodhi tree (*Ficus religiosa*) in the Chinese Garden. OPPOSITE Spectacular circular walkway and viewing platforms descend from the sky in the Cloud Forest Dome.

"Beautifying the rivers and canals requires ingenuity and capital expenditure, but the capital cost of beautifying the city is worth it. It will increase the value of all the buildings along these streams and canals. If we can create water bodies all along the stretches of the rivers and canals, and educate our people not to throw rubbish or litter, we will have a beautiful city. With greening and fishing, we will have something special."

— Lee Kuan Yew, 1977

ABOVE LEFT Named after James MacRitchie, Municipal Engineer from 1883 to 1895, MacRitchie Reservoir is the oldest of the 17 reservoirs. Today, it is a popular spot for hiking and canoeing.

ABOVE RIGHT AND OPPOSITE Bounded by the waters of Upper Seletar Reservoir, the Zoological Gardens are famed for their 'open concept' and tropical floral setting.

Water and Nature

Because Singapore does not have any significant, accessible natural aquifers, water supply has always been an important concern. As early as 1823, British Resident John Crawfurd proposed the building of a reservoir and waterworks to meet the early settlement's water requirements. Unfortunately, for one reason or another, plans kept being shelved, and residents had to wait another 40 years before the first reservoir at Thomson Road was built.

Spearheaded by a donation of S$13,000 from wealthy Straits Chinese merchant Tan Kim Seng, the reservoir was completed in 1867 with the pumps and distributing networks only in working order ten years later. This was 20 years after Tan's philanthropic donation and 14 years after his death in 1864!

Luckily, this slow start to water collection and storage has been progressively expanded over the years, so much so that Singapore now boasts an extensive network of drains, canals, rivers and storm water ponds and 17 reservoirs in total. It still relies on Johor in Malaysia for some of its water needs, but is increasingly looking towards self-reliance in this department. Its water board is also making inroads in desalination and recycling technologies as well.

The four biggest reservoirs — Upper Seletar, Lower Seletar, Peirce and MacRitchie — form part of the Central Catchment Nature Reserve, a conservation area of rainforest, flora and fauna. Not only do they preserve water, they protect a vast amount of bio-diversity as well. Furthermore, they promote outdoor recreation through a network of trails and facilities. There's a wonderful and extensive open-plan zoological gardens and Night Safari zoo; two bird reserves; numerous walking, jogging and cycling trails; facilities for canoeing, kayaking and rowing; and more.

In addition to the central catchment area, the island boasts three other nature reserves — inland at Bukit Timah, and on the coast at Sungei Buloh and Labrador Park — as well as 300 parks, linked by green park connectors, and a number of other outdoor attractions such as gardens, theme parks and underwater parks. For a highly congested city, this is quite a feat.

Green Recreation

Singapore seems to have a zealous belief in the benefits of outdoor recreation. Not only is it seen as a way to keep fit, the government believes that it encourages community activities and fosters national bonding. NParks is constantly updating its website with new linked trails; areas for rowing, kayaking or sailing; campsites and barbecue pits; cycling routes; and more.

Two of the main areas set aside for such purposes are the East Coast Park with its cycling and jogging tracks and Sentosa Island, the latter, somewhat theme-park-esque in its relentless pursuit of the next big ride. With multiple attractions from an outpost of Universal Studios, a luge ride, a zip ride and three beaches, it suffers from over-crowding, especially on the weekends. Having said that, there are still some quiet(er) beaches and areas of tranquility to be found (see page 28).

Cycling has recently seen a gain in popularity, and the extended park connector network is good for both cyclists and walkers. Dragonboat racing on the rivers, sailing off the coast and on Marina Bay, and kayaking on the reservoirs are all options as well.

RIGHT AND OPPOSITE
Clockwise from top left: Sailing has a long history in Singapore and there are more than 10 sailing clubs dotted around the island. Here we see a view of the Marina at Keppel Bay, home to the luxury yacht set. Part of a five-km hiking trail that passes through three major parks — Kent Ridge Park, Telok Blangah Hill Park and Mount Faber Park — is the curvaceous pedestrian Henderson Waves bridge, built in 2008. Cycling at the East Coast Park, a 15-km stretch that follows the coast from Changi in the east to Tanjung Rhu, near the city centre. Jogging track at the multi-purpose National Stadium, which opened its doors in 2014. Luge track on Sentosa island. Catamaran racing on the waters of Marina Bay. A view of one end of Siloso Beach on Sentosa; the three beaches on the island were reclaimed and 'built' using sand bought from Indonesia and Malaysia. The cable car that runs from Mount Faber to Sentosa island.

Heritage Trees

Inaugurated in 2001, Singapore's Heritage Trees Scheme is a conservation programme that protects and promotes the island's mature trees. To date, there are 255 trees on the register — and each is documented according to its age, social, cultural or historical significance, girth and health.

The thinking behind the plan is that urbanization mustn't be allowed to usurp existing green landmarks. It's felt that listing trees and bringing attention to them helps Singaporeans to 'identify with and stay rooted to the place we call home'. Certainly they add to the beauty of the equatorial city-state and also encourage residents to participate in their protection.

A private/government programme, the scheme is open to the public. Anyone can submit an online Heritage Tree nomination, recommending a tree be endorsed. Then NParks' arborists inspect the tree and decide whether the nominated tree is suitable. Qualifying criteria for a tree to be listed as a Heritage Tree includes: a girth (trunk circumference) of more than five metres; and/or botanical, social, historical, cultural and/or aesthetic value.

One of the most famous areas of Heritage Trees is downtown at Connaught Drive where a total of 22 rain trees have been conferred 'Avenue of Heritage Trees' status. Lining the Esplanade they are a magnificent sight. Elsewhere on the island — in the Botanical Gardens, on Pulau Ubin, by the side of a random street — other trees are protected by the scheme. Some have historic or economic significance, such as the rubber or kapok tree; others are simply majestic examples of Mother Nature's bounty.

ABOVE Fort Canning Park contains 25 Heritage Trees. Here we see a massive Ficus shading two ornamental cupolas, designed by George Dromgold Coleman, the first Government Architect and Superintendent of Public Works, who also oversaw work on the park cemetery.

OPPOSITE Clockwise from top left: Heritage Tree avenue of rain trees on Connaught Drive; ficus in the Botanical Gardens; majestic Common Pulai (35m height, 6.4m girth) on Pulau Ubin; Tembusu tree at Bukit Chermin — it appears on Singapore's five-dollar note.

> *To retain the rustic quality and rich heritage of Pulau Ubin, as well as to ensure the safety of existing buildings and structures, agencies are working with stakeholders on a set of design guidelines for restoring or rebuilding buildings and structures on the island.*
>
> — NParks, 2015

Untamed Landscapes

In addition to the multiple parks, reserves and areas of 'managed landscape' are a few much-loved rural areas that have somehow managed to remain — rustic and unmanaged. Sadly, they are always under threat of organisation or demolition.

One such is the 1,000-hectare 'Island of Granite', commonly known as Pulau Ubin. Boomerang-shaped and covered with low hills, it was named for the light blue granite that was mined here and used in much of Singapore's early development. Even though it is only a 10-minute boat ride from Changi Point, it is light years away from urban Singapore in appearance, culture, nature and atmosphere.

Completely undeveloped, emphatically rustic and wholeheartedly individual, Pulau Ubin is a real gem. There's no electricity, piped water or cars, and the few dozen or so families that live there do so in *kampong*-style homes. Relying on fishing, farming or servicing tourists, their numbers are declining. What is not declining, though, is the plentiful forest and grassland, cut through only by gravel roads and tracks. Home to a wide variety of flora and fauna, this has largely replaced the original primary forest habitat.

Visitors to the island are encouraged to come for the day and hire a bike. Many head to Chek Jawa, a conserved wetland area on the east coast of the island, while others are content to walk or cycle in the idyllic interior. Expect to come across wild hog or mousedeer, and plenty of local and migratory birds. Sights of old *kampong* houses, quarries-turned-lakes, abandoned farms and plantations evoke an earlier era. There's a slightly eccentric atmosphere here, all the more evocative as there is nothing else like it in Singapore.

Various scenarios are constantly being bandied around about Pulau Ubin's future: it will be bulldozed like Sentosa and turned into a theme park (worst-case); it will be NParks-ified, or manicured and massaged into yet another tamed green space (middling); it will be left as is (best-case). At the moment, the government is being tight-lipped — much to the relief of nature lovers, the local population and those who don't want to disturb the status quo.

OPPOSITE Clockwise from top left: *Kampong* house on stilts; still, silent and deep, the waters of the old Pekan Quarry; mangroves adjacent Chek Jawa wetlands; Tudor-style House No 1, a weekend home in the 1930s, now a Visitor Centre; Tua Peh Gong Temple, previously worshipped by quarry workers; 'taxi stand' by the main jetty. All Pulau Ubin.

One other rustic area is the land affectionately known as the Green Corridor (Rail Corridor). A lovely 24-kilometre stretch of former railway tracks running from Tanjong Pagar Station in the CBD all the way to the Woodlands Checkpoint, this trail has been likened to New York City's High Line or the Promenade Plantée in Paris. At present it is rustic, slightly dilapidated and utterly charming. People worry that its proposed development (which includes 120 access points, 21 toilet and shower facilities, f&b outlets, as well as bike and jogging tracks) will spoil what is now a beautifully wild and secluded space.

Another area that is currently being redeveloped is Bukit Brown Cemetery. Overgrown and littered with dead leaves, its 200 hectares are home to a quarter of the island's bird species — and the final resting place for more than 100,000 people. Now, a significant portion of those graves have

been exhumed to make way for a highway to relieve congestion — and the government has intimated (though not confirmed) that all its land will be converted into housing by 2030.

The debate pitching 'managed green' versus 'real green' is not a new one: on the one hand, some argue that Singapore needs to accommodate its large population and sentimentality is an indulgence. On the other, the nation celebrates its heritage, and new generations need to be aware of their past to build a better future. Furthermore, nature lovers argue that there are already plenty of 'organized' facilities island-wide: over-manicured Sentosa; the East Coast Park with its jogging, cycle, dining and camping opportunities; multiple trails in the Nature Reserves; and linked walks across the island. They feel there is an argument for abandoning this 'top-down' approach and leaving some parts of the island as Nature intended.

OPPOSITE Four views of the Green Corridor, the old railway bridges and footbridges intact.
ABOVE Graves and shrine at Bukit Brown Cemetery. To many, the graves represent an alternative history of Singapore, one that is based on the true lives of many who worked to make Singapore what it is today.
LEFT A cemetery dog: semi-wild, such dogs live concealed deep within confines of the forest.

EAST
MEETS
WEST

> *The active spirit of enterprise which prevails among all classes is truly astonishing, and for its extent, I believe I may safely say, that no part of the world exhibits a busier scene than the town and environs of Singapore.*
>
> — Stamford Raffles, letter, 30 November 1822

An 1861 painting by artist W Gray (opposite) depicts a panoramic view of Singapore's harbour. A variety of sailing vessels and sampans are bobbing on the calm waters of the port city while, in the background, stands a neat waterfront of colonial edifices with strategic Fort Canning Hill behind.

In only 40 years, the little dot at the tip of the Malay Peninsula had been transformed. Sir Thomas Stamford Raffles' aim to fashion Singapore into 'the Grandest Emporium the Far East, nay the World, had yet known' had proved to be no idle boast. The potential he saw in the island's location and deep natural harbour had been furthered by Singapore's free port status, its low taxation and plentiful immigration.

This waterfront view is probably a pretty accurate picture of the fledgling colony. Singapore attracted fleets of ships carrying goods from all over the world; with them came a variety of merchants, traders, civil servants, labourers and more, all lured by the promise of an Emporium-city that could deliver a life many had only dreamed of. Even though the majority came from China, there were Arabs, Armenians and Jews from today's Middle East; Malays, Bugis and Javanese from closer to home; a variety of Europeans; Bengalis, Parsees and Tamils from India; and more.

By the early 1860s, Singapore was a thriving port city that came to dominate the region. It was a melting pot of different ethnicities and nationalities — each and every soul jostling for a piece of the proverbial pie. Even though many had arrived, thinking they would work for a while, then go 'home', the lure of their lifestyles proved irresistible. This ever-growing and varied population set down roots, bought land or homes, married, and had children. Over time, they became the ancestors of today's multi-cultural Singaporean citizens.

PREVIOUS PAGE 'View from Government Hill', 1837, by the artist W C Smith shows the early settlement lining the sea-shore, Fort Canning in the background, and a number of different people of different ethnicities in the foreground.

OPPOSITE W Gray's mid 19th-century view of the harbour gives a clear view of the fledgling settlement: Raffles Institution is found directly below the flagstaff; to its right are Beach Road houses; St Andrew's Cathedral is clearly seen; and further left is the Padang.

The Chinese

From the very beginning, the Chinese have been central to Singapore's success. The first immigrants came from the nearby region: Penang, Malacca, Medan, the Javanese ports of Batavia and Surabaya and various islands in the Riau archipelago. Many of these were Straits-born (or Peranakan) Chinese, from merchant communities who had settled previously in Nanyang or the 'Southern Seas'.

They were followed in increasing numbers by Chinese from China itself. For the most part the incomers comprised poor farmers, labourers or craftsmen seeking a better life in Nanyang. The first junk from Amoy arrived in February 1821, and this was followed by boatloads of (mostly) men from the southern coast of China. The largest group comprised Hokkiens from Fujian province, but there were many others — Cantonese from Guangdong, nomadic Hakkas from northern

Guangdong, Teochews from Shantou, Kwongsais from Guangzi, Hokchius from Fuzhou and the Hainanese from Hainan island.

As these early settlers arrived in sailing ships, they worshipped one of the patron deities of the Taoist pantheon, the protectress of sailors called Ma Zhu. Her idol was at the Thian Hock Kheng Temple (first built 1821–2), so this was often the first port of call for new arrivals. Situated on the waterfront on Telok Ayer Street, it was conveniently located. Newcomers would then head to the *kongsi* or clan association, an organization that comprised a group of individuals that spoke the same dialect or came from the same province in China. These clan associations helped new arrivals with employment, accommodation and the like.

Many found work as 'coolies' — indentured labourers in any manner of employment from plantation and farm work to construction, work at the docks and as rickshaw pullers. Their lives were extremely hard: living conditions were squalid; wages meager; and many found solace in opium and gambling. Nevertheless, they continued to arrive on Singapore's shores, willing to take on gruelling work because they thought the colony offered them a future.

They were right. Today's Singaporeans owe a huge debt to these early immigrants as they formed the backbone of the early colony's economy — and enabled future generations to prosper.

OPPOSITE AND ABOVE Four views of Thian Hock Keng Temple (completed 1842), the most important Hokkien temple in Singapore. Built in traditional southern Chinese architectural style, the entire structure was assembled without nails. It has been restored several times over the years.

> *How I wish I could convey an idea, however faint, of this huge, mingled, coloured, busy, Oriental population …and of the resistless, overpowering, astonishing Chinese element, which is gradually turning Singapore into a Chinese city!*

— Isabella Bird,
The Golden Chersonese and the Way Thither, 1883

Ethnic Chinese make up 75 percent of today's Singaporean population, ie roughly three out of every four people is ethnically Chinese. Between 1840 and 1900 about two and a half million people left mainland China to find jobs wherever they could. Many thousands of such *sinkeh* ('new arrivals' in Hokkien) ended up in Singapore — and never left.

This population increase and the opening of the Suez Canal in 1869, a factor that had huge repercussions on Singapore's import and export volume, resulted in Raffles' original Chinatown proving inadequate for the growing population. It expanded from the Telok Ayer and Amoy Street area towards Commercial Square (Raffles Place) and Boat Quay, and later moved further north and westwards to Bukit Pasoh and Tanjong Pagar. To this day, it remains roughly in the same place.

The architecture of Chinatown's shophouses was strongly influenced by southern Fujian architecture and was originally fairly rudimentary in style. Built as merchants' dwellings, with a shop at ground level and living quarters above, plots were long and thin and each house shared a party wall with its neighbours. A 'five-foot-way' — the minimum width stipulated by the building regulations of the time — was situated at the front, and there was usually a courtyard at the back for cooking, ventilation and the like.

Over time, as Chinatown became ever more crowded, these dwellings were divided and sub-divided again to accommodate the ever-increasing population. Wealthier and usually second-generation Chinese families began to move away from the centre of town, building similar types of houses, but in more salubrious areas. The shop was replaced by a reception room, the structures became deeper, and a second court was often incorporated into the plan. Facades were richly ornamented in a variety of styles, with inspiration mainly coming from China in the form of stucco reliefs and painted decorative panels.

Chinatown itself remained the hub for Chinese trades — and continued to remain so until as recently as a couple of decades ago.

OPPOSITE Every part of the Chinese shophouse has its idiosyncracies, a fact that makes these buildings so appealing. Windows are a case in point. Here we see two types of upper-storey windows: the top one is probably earlier as it features Chinese decoration above the panes. The lower one is more Classical in inspiration with fanlights above the windows, and Rococco-style stucco work on pillars.

Chinese Poor

Most 19th-century Chinese immigrants lived in cramped cubby-hole 'rooms' in sub-divided shophouses. The Chinatown Heritage Centre, located in three shophouses on Pagoda Street, gives a thoughtfully-presented taste of their professions, hobbies and domestic lives.

Chinese Rich

Every immigrant to Singapore dreamed of wealth, prestige and power. Some got it. They moved to the suburbs, often building palatial homes like the one featured in this painting below. The Peranakan Museum showcases the splendour in which they lived; we give you a taste of their tastes here.

BELOW From left to right: Chinatown Heritage Centre has imaginatively recreated the original interiors of its shophouse tenants in the 1950s. The experience is aided by ambient soundscapes and audio conversations. Shrines with joss sticks and offerings to the Gods are placed in the five-foot-way. A Chinese letter writer at work. Practical 'interior design' in a tailor's work space. A barber's 'shop' in the teeming five-foot-way. The kitchen, adjacent the lightwell, was shared by tenants and featured a charcoal hearth or *dapur*. A tailor's shop with original cabinetry, cloth, sewing machine and patterns.

BELOW From left to right: Oil painting by A L Wilson depicting the Amber Road mansion of Lee Cheng Yan, a wealthy Straits Chinese businessman. Designed by Lermit & Westerhout in 1902, it was lived in by the same family for over seven decades. Sadly, it was demolished in 1983. Recreated kitchen with *kopitiam* table and bentwood chairs, charcoal hearth and 'meat-safe'. Peranakan bridal bed, with embroidered drapes and hanging lucky talismans. Hand-painted outdoor lantern. Heavy, intricately carved, Chinese altar that has been adapted with the addition of a Christian scene; many Perankans were Christian but continued to practise ancestor worship. Airy lightwell. Heavy rosewood furniture inlaid with mother-of-pearl.

The Malay World

When Raffles first 'discovered' Singapore, there were a few isolated settlements of mainly fisherfolk along the fringes of the island, as well as a few farming communities inland. But, with development came an influx of people from the immediate surroundings — Malays from the Malay Peninsula, Sumatra and the Riau archipelago and Javanese, Boyanese and Bugis from the Dutch East Indies.

Attracted by the business opportunities offered by the colonial authorities, many Malays traded in so-called Straits' goods (spices, cloth, minerals, essential oils, for example), while others became shopkeepers, craftsmen, labourers and farmers, amongst other professions.

Kampong Glam was the area allocated to the Malays. Translating as 'Village of the Gelam Tree', the area was given to the Malay ruler of Singapore at the time, Sultan Hussein Mohamed Shah, and 600 of his family members, when he ceded the island of Singapura to the British. Even though there don't appear to be any *Melaleuca leucadendron* or *gelam* trees in the area today, presumably there were in the past.

In addition to the Sultan and his entourage, there was also a population of Bugis, Arabs, Javanese and Boyanese as well as a number of Chinese Muslims. Raffles himself donated $3,000 for the building of a 'respectable mosque' which served the community until 1924 when the current Sultan Mosque was built. Then, as now,

ABOVE The Sultan Mosque is the spiritual centre for Singapore's Muslim community. It was built in 1924–26 to a design by Denis Santry of Swan & Maclaren in Saracenic style, inspired by Classical, Persian, Moorish and Turkish elements. A Public Monument, it was recently restored in 2016.

OPPOSITE Kampong Glam is home to some of Singapore's earliest shophouses. Built in what is called the simple Early Style, they are characterised by minimal ornamentation and low ceiling heights. The ones on Haji Lane used to house pilgrims transitting through Singapore en route to Mecca.

it was a colourful area of small streets lined with shophouses. In addition to the Malays, Yemeni traders manned a myriad of fabric and carpet stores spilling out into the streets, while other shops sold perfumes and religious paraphernalia from Arabia. Many Javanese were leather and metal craftsmen, while the Bugis and Boyanese often worked in boatyards lining the Kallang River.

Many streets were known for particular trades. North Bridge Road was home to tailors and Chinese-run goldsmith shops, while Sultan Gate used to be dominated by stonemasons and blacksmiths. Before land reclamation, the Beach Road waterfront was the focal point for trading and shipping services and Haji Lane, named after the Hajj or pilgrimage undertaken by

Muslims to Mecca and Medina, housed centres for pilgrimage brokers who organised Hajj trips for Muslim pilgrims from around the region.

A stroll around Kampong Glam today allows visitors to re-imagine these earlier times. The old Sultan's palace, adjacent the mosque, houses a museum cum cultural centre, while Muslim coffee shops and eateries line the streets. Those in search of Javanese batiks and checked *longyis* won't be disappointed and there is also a slew of craft and curio shops selling jewellery, baskets, carpets, rattan and leather wares. The area is also home to a number of independent fashion boutiques and funky restaurants, cafés and bars. Gentrification has brought change, but much of the old atmosphere remains.

"The native streets monopolize the picturesqueness of Singapore with their bizarre crowds, but more interesting still are the bazaars or continuous rows of open shops which create for themselves a perpetual twilight by hanging tatties or other screens outside the sidewalks, forming long shady alleys, in which crowds of buyers and sellers chaffer over their goods... Chinese joss-houses, Hindu temples, and Mohammedan mosques almost jostle each other, and the indescribable clamour of the temples and the din of the joss-houses are faintly pierced by the shrill cry from the minarets calling the faithful to prayer, and proclaiming the divine unity and the mission of Mahomet in one breath."

— Isabella Bird,
The Golden Chersonese and the Way Thither, 1883

OPPOSITE The area around Haji Lane has become the meeting point for the anti-shopping mall crowd. Cafés and bars alternate with fashionista boutiques and trendy design stores, while graffiti enlivens walls. Meanwhile, tradition continues in the shops selling prayer carpets and textiles, as well as sarong, *kebaya* and jewellery. It's also the place for inexpensive Middle Eastern coffee and cuisine.

The Singapore River

The opening of the Suez Canal in 1869, the evolution of the steamship and Singapore's inclusion as an important station in the British Empire's network of submarine telegraph lines all contributed to Singapore's growth. The original city clustered around the Singapore River began to expand — westwards towards New (later Keppel) Harbour, east towards the East Coast and Katong, and north along River Valley Road and Orchard Road towards Bukit Timah.

The outer areas tended to house the more wealthy bourgeoisie, both Asian and European, while the inner core remained home to the multitude of workers. Binding this mercantile community was the beating pulse of the city — the Singapore River.

Trade was, after all, Singapore's *raison d'etre*. Numerous early photographs and paintings depict the teeming waterways and quays with flotillas of boats, workmen loading and unloading goods in bumboats, and rows of godowns, warehouses and jetties. Boat Quay

housed the settlement's first trading houses, but by the 1860s development extended upstream to Clarke and Robertson Quays. By the late 1890s there was an assortment of godowns, ricemills, sawmills, boatyards and other industries along the upper reaches as well.

Today, the river is again a hub, albeit of a different nature. The harbour has moved westwards, the riverbanks have been repaired, the pollution from up-river has been attended to, and many of the quayside row houses have been transformed into shops, clubs, bars and restaurants. The area's regeneration has ensured a steady flow of visitors, the only difference being that today's residents and tourists come to play — not work.

BELOW Lithograph of the Singapore River, probably dating from the 1860s. The bridge in the far distance is the Elgin Bridge, built in 1862.

OPPOSITE Three contemporary views of the river show the mix of early architecture (and bridges) backed by the towers of the Central Business District.

> *We, the citizens of Singapore,*
> *pledge ourselves as one united people,*
> *regardless of race, language or religion,*
> *to build a democratic society*
> *based on justice and equality*
> *so as to achieve happiness, prosperity*
> *and progress for our nation.*
>
> — Sinnathamby Rajaratnam, 1966

The Indians in Singapore

In May 2015, at the opening of the new Indian Heritage Centre in Singapore's 'Little India', Prime Minister Lee Hsien Loong noted that the Indian community had contributed to Singapore 'in deep ways'. Currently comprising about nine percent of the country's citizens and permanent residents, Indians form Singapore's third largest ethnic group.

Indian traders had established trade links with South East Asia well before Singapore was founded, but with the settlement's inception in the 19th century, there came an influx of mainly South Indians, most of whom were labourers or traders, as well as some convict labourers. Records from 1821 indicated there were 132 Indians living on the island; by 1860, there were about 13,000, most of whom were Tamils.

At the time, they tended to live near their work places — the *chettiars* or moneychangers and shopkeepers around the mercantile Raffles Place and the labourers near the docks or railways. In time, some Tamil shopkeepers migrated to the Serangoon Road area, as did workers in the brick kilns and cattle industries. This resulted in the formation of the ethnic enclave today known as Little India.

Even though Little India is a magnet for tourists, it somehow seems more authentic than Chinatown. One really can imagine oneself in the subcontinent here: a maze of shophouse lanes radiates out from Serangoon Road, each populated by sari, silver and gold shops; vegetable and flower stalls; Indian DVD and music stores; local curry houses; and more. The scent of jasmine garlands mingles with cumin, *roti prata* and Ayurvedic oils, while Indian *bhangra*, Bollywood music and the clang of temple bells are ever present. Young Indian men promenade Little India's alleys on the weekends, while bargain hunters flock to the 24-hour Mustafa Centre, the king of Singapore's white goods' stores. Dawn sees the immense Tekka wet market bustling with herb, vegetable and other vendors catering to all and sundry.

Over the years, the Indian community has grown in strength and numbers. Notable pioneers include government founding member Sinnathamby Rajaratnam (1915–2006) who composed Singapore's national pledge (above) and numerous other government ministers (including two Presidents). Today, one finds many prominent Indians in the civil service and in business, culture and the arts.

OPPOSITE TOP Slightly atypical shophouse row on Norris street, as the structure on left stands out with its North Indian temple architecture. It was originally a school built by the Ramakrishna Mission.

OPPOSITE BELOW Upper-floor windows of one of the last surviving Chinese mansions in Little India. It was built in 1900 by Tan Teng Niah, the owner of a rubber smokehouse, for his wife.

ABOVE Clockwise from top left: A newsstand close to Serangoon road, selling newspapers and gossip magazines from India. A Ganesh statue on the wall of a vegetable seller's stall. With his easily identifiable elephant head, Ganesh is one of the most loved of the Hindu deities. Shophouse five-foot-way turned vegetable market. A flower seller: marigold, jasmine and orchids are made into garlands, while chrysanthemums and rose petals are sold separately.

ABOVE Clockwise from top left: Flowers are used both as offerings and to scent homes and cars. The first two photos depict jasmine garlands, while on right we see a bunch of lotus blooms. Assortment of Hindu deity statues atop the roof of the Sri Veeramakaliamman Temple, built by Tamils in South Indian style. Anybody need onions? Umbrella tree installation by Marthalia Budiman — an entrant in an Urban Redevelopment Authority competition entitled 'My Ideas for Public Spaces: Forgotten Spaces'. Visitors are encouraged to rest in the shade beneath these colourful 'trees'.

> *Emerald Hill's reputation as an exclusive residential neighbourhood for Singapore's Peranakan élite in the first two decades of the last century is reflected in the quality of its architecture: tall Baroque townhouses set back from the street, most of them designed by the leading architects of the day.*
> — Julian Davison, *Singapore Shophouse*, 2010

The Peranakan Community

The term 'Peranakan' (translating as 'local born') refers to people of mixed Chinese and Malay/Indonesian heritage. Peranakans are descendents of Chinese immigrant traders who travelled (and later settled) in Nanyang from the 14th century onwards and married local Malay women or Bataks from Sumatra. Their offspring, and succeeding generations, were also known as Straits Chinese, as many were born in the British-controlled Straits Settlements of Malacca, Penang and Singapore.

The men were known as *babas*, the women as *nyonyas* — and they consciously allied themselves with the English in Singapore to differentiate themselves from the other Chinese who were generally of a lower socio-economic class. Many early Peranakans were extremely entrepreneurial. Acting as traders, shopkeepers, in real estate, shipping and the banking world, and later as landowners and planters, they very quickly grew in prominence.

This singular group of people eventually became very influential in the region — amassing on the way a whole range of cultural practices and traditions that are unique. In addition to English, Peranakans spoke a patois Malay that contained plenty of Hokkien words and phrases; they dressed in a mix of English, Malay and Chinese costume; their cuisine was lauded, integrating as it did Chinese styles with local Indonesian and Malay ingredients; and their architecture and interior design was particularly striking. In terms of religion, many embraced Christianity, but retained the Chinese practice of ancestor worship.

In Singapore, the Peranakans' heyday came between the wars. Settled in comfortable terraced homes in salubrious areas or in vast mansions in the suburbs, their lifestyles were lavish, their place in society assured. Luckily, many former Peranakan areas have been gazetted for conservation, so a stroll around Emerald Hill or Joo Chiat in Katong, for example, gives a flavour of Peranakan life. Joo Chiat, named after landowner and philanthropist Chew Joo Chiat (1857–1926), is famed for its many bakeries specialising in Nyonya cakes and its rows of terrace houses are particularly colourful.

OPPOSITE Clockwise from top left: A corner shophouse on Joo Chiat Road painted a vibrant red. Two so-called 'barrack houses' — part row-house, part Anglo-Malay style as they are raised a little off the ground. There are two remaining streets with this type of house in Katong. A pair of *pintu pagar* doors open out on to an Emerald Hill five-foot-way. A particularly pristine corner shophouse in the Joo Chiat area. Ornately carved entrance to the Baba House, a rich *towkay*'s townhouse built at the turn of the last century, now open to the public as a museum. Emerald Hill blue-and-white home behind a bottlebrush tree.

The Arabs in Singapore

Most Arabs who settled in South East Asia, including Singapore, were from the Hadhramaut region in the Yemen and thus came to be known as 'Hadhramis'. Most of them have close family ties with Yemen even now — something that is increasingly unsettling for them when one considers the current conflicts there.

From the mid-18th century onwards, Arab traders had made their way to Asia with many settling in the then Dutch East Indies. With the new trading post in Singapore, some shifted over (and others came directly from Yemen), so that the community became an integral part of society engaging in trade, shipping, plantation estates and organizing Hajj pilgrimages. It also contributed generously in establishing mosques, religious schools and other charitable organisations in Singapore. With the spread of Islam in South East Asia, Hadhramis came to be custodians of the religion amongst the local Muslim communities.

Many Arabs intermarried and intermingled with the Malay community, so much so that many lost their fluency in Arabic and began to consider themselves Malay. The Arab Association in Singapore called the Alwehdah, a voluntary charitable organization, has tried to reunite such people with their roots; it also provides welfare services and seeks to promote Islam.

Evidence of this strong Arab influence is seen all over the city-state: names such as Aljunied, Alkaff and Alsagoff have become important landmarks in Singapore's landscape, with mosques, streets, hospitals and more bearing their names.

OPPOSITE Masjid Alkaff Kampung Melayu, near Bedok Reservoir, replaced the original mosque built by the Alkaff family in 1932.

ABOVE Clockwise from top left: Tudor-style Alkaff Mansion, built by the Alkaff family as a weekend home on Telok Blangah in 1918. It was famous for its lavish entertainment, and is now a restaurant. Typical coffee and snacks, Arab-style, in Kampong Glam. Three shops in Kampong Glam: Silks, cushions and carpets and ornamental hanging lamps are some of the Arabic wares on offer here.

The Eurasians

When Jacob Schooling won the 100 metres butterfly in the 2016 Olympic Games in Rio de Janeiro, he put the spotlight on Singapore's Eurasian community, a group that has contributed significantly to the growth and wealth of the country.

As the name suggests, Eurasians are generally descendents of a marital union between an Asian and a European, in this case a European who came out East during the Portuguese, Dutch or British colonial eras. They were amongst the first of the settlers in Singapore; early Eurasian family names include Ferrao (1820), Dias (1821), D'Almeida (1825), Leicester (1826–27), Woodford (1836), McIntyre (1939), Sequeira (1837), Oliveiro (1844), Gomes (1949), De Rozario (1849) and Clarke (1850s) to name a few. Some other Eurasians are descended from other European races.

In 19th-century Singapore, Eurasians often acted as a bridge between the Europeans and locals, as many were Christian and they frequently spoke good English. Many men served as clerks in the civil service, banks and trading houses, while a substantial number of Eurasian women worked as teachers or nurses. During the last century, there have been many Eurasians in government, including Benjamin Sheares who served as President from 1971 to 1981.

Eurasians have also contributed significantly to the cultural and artistic life of Singapore. Jeremy Monteiro, for example, is a famous jazz musician, while Rex Shelley was an award-winning writer, known for his works about the Eurasian communities in Singapore and Malaysia. Even today, there is an active Eurasian Association whose mission is to 'enrich the legacy of our cohesive and vibrant Eurasian community that is integrated with and contributing to a multi-ethnic, multi-religious and multi-cultural Singapore'.

LEFT Clockwise from top: A blue-and-white tile fresco at the Eurasian Association in Singapore depicting Portuguese ships departing Lisboa harbour en route to trade in Asia. Many Eurasians are descended from such seafarers. The entrance to the Singapore Recreation Club, a social and sporting club set up by 30 Eurasians in 1883 on Waterloo Street. It later moved to the Padang. Slices of sugee cake, a sponge cake with almonds loved by Eurasians.

The Armenians

Armenians are another small but successful community in Singapore. Their numbers were small (in the 1880s at their most prolific they numbered fewer than 100 families), but their influence was large. Although they arrived as traders, many diversified into different professions — the law, the press and hoteliering, amongst others. Today, remaining landmarks of the Armenians include the Church of St Gregory the Illuminator near Raffles Hotel and several streets, including Armenian Street, Galiston Avenue, Sarkies Road and St Martin's Drive.

Other reminders of the Armenian presence include Raffles Hotel (built and run by the entrepreneurial Sarkies Brothers whose hotel business stretched across the whole of Asia); the *Straits Times* (co-founded by one Catchick Moses who moved to Singapore from Penang); and Singapore's national flower, the Vanda Miss Joaquim (a hybrid orchid propagated by a botanist by the name of Ms Vanda Joaquim).

ABOVE Clockwise from left: The spire of the Armenian Church, commissioned by the first 12 Armenian families that settled in Singapore. It opened in 1836 to a design by George Drumgoole Coleman. Handsome corner building on Armenian Street with deco flagpole. The Vanda Miss Joaquim hybrid orchid.

The Jewish Community

In the 19th century, a small number of Jewish traders and merchants settled in Singapore, as the Settlement offered both religious freedom and economic opportunity. Over the subsequent 200 years, their influence and identity have far outreached their small(ish) numbers.

The first Jews to settle in Singapore were of Baghdadi origin and mainly came via India where they had settled to escape harassment by the then Wali of Baghdad. They quickly prospered in the import/export businesses of spices, cotton goods, coffee, timber and the legalized opium trade. The 1846 census notes that six of the then 43 merchant houses were owned by Jews. In the latter half of the 19th century, they were joined by groups of Ashkenazi Jews fleeing persecution in Germany, Poland and Russia.

Because of fluctuations in the price of opium, many early Jews followed the example of their counterparts in India and started to invest in real estate. Many settled in the so-called Jewish quarter or *mahallah* ('place' in Arabic) around Middle, Wilkie, Sophia and Selegie roads, where prominent Stars of David still remain on some of the buildings. The more affluent built homes by the sea in the eastern suburbs where a few roads bear Jewish names — Meyer, Amber and Elias, for example.

Even though it is difficult to recapture the lives of these early pioneers, many of their names live on in the fabric of Singapore today: Manasseh Meyer (1843–1930), whose firm built and/or owned the Adelphi and Sea View hotels, Meyer Mansions, Meyer Flats and the Crescent Flats apartments, as well as two palatial residences, Killiney House and Jeshurun, the latter located on Meyer Road; doctor and botanist, Nathaniel Wallich, the designer of Singapore's first botanical garden; renowned businessman Nissim Nissim Adis, the owner of the Grand Hotel de l'Europe, amongst others. Later David Marshall, a Jew of Iraqi origin, became the first Chief Minister of the Republic of Singapore, while Dr Yayah Cohen became Surgeon General.

> *We have a small number here ... they have a synagogue in the Chinese town, just a shophouse that they use, and it is here that you may see their patriarch Abraham Solomon who not only leads their community in the promised land but indeed looks exactly I am sure as Moses looked — tall with long flowing robes, a turban and a great white beard.*
>
> — Early resident, Benjamin Cook, letter, 24 December 1854

ABOVE LEFT Signage on the David Elias Building (1928) designed by Swan & Maclaren for a Jewish merchant to house his trading company.

OPPOSITE AND ABOVE RIGHT Interior views and outside plaque at the Renaissance-style Chesed-El Synagogue, built with funds from Menasseh Meyer.

WAR
AND
PEACE

Singapore commemorates its war dead in sensitive and imaginative ways — through memorials, museums, chapels and churchyards. This chapter gives an overview of World Wars I and II, and the physical reminders of those turbulent days.

For most of its history, Singapore has been relatively free from strife. In its early incarnations as Temasek and Singapura, it was a cog in the wheels of Far East trade, then after Raffles' landing, its energies were focused on building and expansion. Once the 20th century came round, it was relatively prosperous and peaceful.

From 1918 to the outbreak of World War I, it grew from a tiny outpost at the tip of Malaya to become an economic powerhouse at the crossroads of Asia/Europe trade. Even though it was extremely successful from a material point of view, it did lag behind in terms of education, social services, sanitation, housing and the like (compared to Western nations).

This began to change at the turn of the century as 'modernism' began to be felt: improvements in technologies and communications (the advent of the motor car; the beginnings of air traffic; electrification of the town with street lights and electricity in homes; the introduction of the radio) resulted in significant changes. If it had not been for the outbreak of World War I and the Great Depression afterwards, the colony would have continued to prosper.

These, along with the Indian Sepoy Mutiny of 1915, resulted in a falling-off of trade, higher prices for basic foodstuffs and a decade or more of economic hardship. The massive decline in exports of tin and rubber particularly affected Singapore. As a response, the colonial authorities introduced quotas on the number of Chinese immigrants, shored up the defences of the colony, and sat back while some of its inhabitants returned to their countries of birth. Essentially, as with the rest of the world, Singapore readjusted its sights.

After the 1930s, the economy began to pick up — and there is no doubt this trend would have continued had it not been for the outbreak of World War II.

PREVIOUS PAGE Rows of white gravestones at the Kranji War Memorial, often inscribed with the words 'Buried near this spot', are a poignant reminder of the fact that many of the soldiers that died in World War II were not given proper burial.

OPPOSITE Designed by architect Denis Santry of Swan & Maclaren, the Singapore Cenotaph was modelled after the 1920 Sir Edwin Lutyens' Whitehall Cenotaph in London. The inscription on the reverse side of the Cenotaph is brief, but revealing. No names are listed, but the simple phrase 'They died so we might live' is carved in Singapore's four main languages: English, Malay, Chinese and Tamil. It is located in Esplanade Park along Connaught Drive.

Britain's 'impregnable fortress' surrendered to the Japanese on 15 February 1942. Prime Minister Winston Churchill described the fall of Singapore as 'the worst disaster and largest capitulation in British history'.

Mementoes of War and Occupation

The story of how 'Fortress Singapore' capitulated to the Japanese a mere 70 days after they landed in Malaya has been told countless times — and needs no further elucidation here. Suffice it to say that this 'bastion of British might' (as one English newspaper described it) was overpowered (despite some spirited resistance) — and on 15 February 1942 the British authorities surrendered to the Japanese, who proceeded to occupy Singapore for the next three and a half years.

Approximately 85,000 British and Australian troops were captured, many of whom went on to endure forced labour posts on the Siam-Burma railway and elsewhere. Many died in captivity. Singaporeans fared no better, with thousands of Chinese killed and other ethnic groups such as Malays and Indians not spared either. The

hardships of the Occupation were manifold. A visit to the military museum at Fort Siloso on the northwestern tip of Sentosa is a must for those interested in this period. Built in the 1880s to aid in the protection of the port, particularly the entrance to Keppel Harbour, Fort Siloso was an important part of Singapore's coastal defence. Much of the original fortification on Mount Siloso remains, but there are also added attractions that showcase the life of a military man in the late 1800s and early 1900s.

Also of interest may be the Images of Singapore museum housed in one of Sentosa's former military buildings. Through multimedia displays, screened theatre presentations and lifesize tableaux, it offers a chronological history of Singapore from the earliest days to the present. The sections on World War II and the Japanese Occupation are particularly effective.

ABOVE One of four coastal gun batteries on Sentosa, Fort Siloso has been reconstructed to showcase life as it was leading up to World War II. The Surrender Gallery features waxworks produced in 1972 to mark the two main surrender ceremonies.

ABOVE Clockwise from top left: A guardpost at Fort Siloso. The art deco facade of the Fort Motor Factory where the British surrendered to the Japanese. Two paintings/sketches of life in the Occupation and a signpost at the Memories at Old Ford Factory museum.

Many other mementoes remain today in Singapore to remind the populace and visitors of the grim days of war and occupation. The venue of the British surrender at the Ford Factory on Upper Bukit Timah Road features an exhibition gallery showcasing life during the Japanese Occupation, while the underground command centre of the British forces in Fort Canning Hill, part of the headquarters of the Malaya Command, has been turned into a museum called the Battlebox. Here, the 'Battlebox Tour: A Story of Strategy and Surrender', tells two stories — that of the fall of Malaya and Singapore in World War II, and how an underground command centre functioned during the war.

A visit to Changi Village also has some pertinent reminders of World War II. Variously the site for coconut, sago and rubber plantations, a self-contained artillery base from 1927 to 1942, massacres and internment by the Japanese during the Occupation and a Royal Air Force base after the war, it is a curious mix. Some of the old colonial barracks remain, as does one of the three 15-inch 'monster' guns installed to counter Japan's naval strength. Found at the Johor Battery, named in appreciation of Sultan Ibrahim of Johor's donation of £500,000 as a Silver Jubilee gift for King George V for the British war campaign, it still startles by its sheer enormity.

Nearby is an extremely moving, albeit small, exhibition space at the Changi Museum, featuring letters, drawings, photographs and personal artefacts of some of the POWs who were held in captivity at nearby Changi Prison. The museum acts both as an educational resource centre and a site for POWs and their families to reflect (and hopefully gain closure) on the many emotional scars inflicted by the war years. It also contains a small chapel and replicas of the famous Changi Murals, a set of biblical themed frescoes that were painted by Stanley Warren, a British bombardier and POW.

ABOVE A replica of a 15-inch gun and 800kg shell at the Johor Battery near Changi Village. Designed as one of Singapore's reminders of the war, the historical site was officially launched on 15 February 2002 as part of a commemorative programme for the 60th anniversary of the fall of Singapore. This event was witnessed by 200 returning POWs, their friends and family members.

ABOVE Entrance to the
Changi Chapel and exhibits
at the Changi Museum,
including one of the so-
called Changi Murals.

LEFT Exterior of the bungalow with a battle scene mural at the Reflections at Bukit Chandu centre.

Little visited, but definitely worth the effort, is the Reflections at Bukit Chandu interpretative centre housed in a colonial bungalow near the site of the Battle of Pasir Panjang, a defining battle between the 1,400-strong soldiers of the Malay Regiment and the 13,000-strong Japanese army. Their heroic last stand is presented through artefacts, exhibits and multimedia displays.

Most emotional of all, however, may be the Kranji War Memorial and Cemetery, situated in a rural spot in the far north of the island. Managed by the Commonwealth War Graves Commission, it commemorates the 24,000 Allied soldiers who died during World War II. Beautifully maintained, it presents serried ranks of crosses and a monolithic memorial etched with the names of the various regiments, all within a peaceful green environment that encourages quiet contemplation. Annual services are held here on ANZAC Day and Remembrance Day, giving people an opportunity to honour the memory of the fallen. At other times, it is simply kept open for those who want to pay their respects.

OPPOSITE TOP The Japanese Cemetery Park contains 910 tombstones, as well as memorials to Japanese military casualties and executed war criminals.

OPPOSITE BOTTOM Three views of the Alexandra Hospital, a British Military Hospital and site of a massacre during World War II.

ABOVE The idyllic surrounds of Fort Canning Park contain plenty of reminders of Singapore's war history. On left is the entrance to the Far East Command Centre and on right is one of a pair of 9-pound canons that sit adjacent to South Battery, the main gun battery for the island's defence.

*British, Australians, New Zealanders, Indians, Chinese
and Malays. An international assortment of many races
Fought for a land so defensively stark
A noble calling not for faint hearts.*

— from the poem 'Tribute to Heroes', LTC Andy Tan, 2005

ABOVE The sober white structures and lawns of the Kranji War Memorial contain the graves of thousands of Allied troops. Many of the headstones are inscribed simply with the words 'a soldier of the 1939–1945 war'. The walls contain names of over 25,000 men and women who died in Malaya during the war.

SINGAPORE
STYLE

> *The Singapore design industry may be young, but the breadth of work over the last five decades is testament to its effervescent growth and tenacity.*
>
> — Jeffrey Ho, DesignSingapore Council, 2015

Nearly 200 years after Sir Stamford Raffles landed on what is affectionately called Asia's 'Little Red Dot', the island has been transformed beyond imagination. What was once untamed territory is now a hugely successful country with a vibrant and dynamic creative culture: the built environment is innovative; the equatorial landscape is part and parcel of the city; and everywhere we see the results of an imaginative design scene.

Of course the phrase 'Singapore Style' is an overused one, but what it means in this chapter is a brief summing-up of national (artistic, cultural and commercial) identity. It gives visitors some 'must-see' sights and residents a sense of pride in what they've achieved in a relatively short span of time. Many of the topics covered are quirky vignettes of the city-state's character — they celebrate art, sculpture, theatre and design; architectural heritage re-use and new-builds; traditional habits and lifestyles; local brands and companies; and more.

In the 19th and much of the 20th century, Singapore was rather a racy place. Risqué song-and-dance shows were part of the Great World Entertainment centres; opium dens were two-a-penny in Chinatown, with opium sales only outlawed in the 1940s; Bugis Junction was well known to sailors the world over as the place where both Asian and European girls plied their trade; Smith Street, then Keong Saik Road, were notorious red-light districts (and some brothels are still in existence there); and there's always been a healthy 'ladyboy' culture.

It's difficult to pinpoint exactly when this ribaldry began to diminish, but with the advent of 'straitlaced Singapore' and the 'Fine City' (where apparently you could be fined for literally anything!), there was certainly an easing out of such fun and frolics. Thankfully, the last couple of decades have seen a relaxing of certain 'serious Singapore' rules and regulations — and with this generally more laissez-faire and tolerant climate has come a resurgence of creativity.

As a result, Singapore is now home to a thriving artistic and design scene. Its architects are known the world over; new technologies have spear-headed growth in interior, product and graphic design; art, music, theatre and dance is thriving; and collaborations across disciplines have led to a revival of the nation's entrepreneurial spirit. Growing confidence — and international recognition — has perhaps resulted in a 'return to roots'. This isn't a nostalgic yearning for the past; more a pride in history and heritage, and an active reinvention of both.

PREVIOUS PAGE In the Blair Plain district a nostalgic mural depicts the weekly wash in days gone by.

OPPOSITE Ministry of Design's funky entranceway to COO, a new-meets-old hostel in Tiong Bahru.

> *We celebrate excellence in the arts and work to make [art] accessible to all. We believe the arts to be a vital avenue for self-expression, learning and reflection, and are constantly striving to create a sustainable environment within which the arts can thrive.*
>
> — National Arts Council Mission

ABOVE Clockwise from left: Gold filigree metal and glass entrance to the National Gallery. The conversion was completed in 2015 by French firm, StudioMilou. Renovated interior of the court house building. Padang atrium where a series of gigantic metal trees supports the glass and metal roof. Warm-toned titanium and glass coated wing of the Asian Civilisations Museum merges with the original 19th-century building. View from inside the National Gallery over the Padang to the three-towers of MBS.

OPPOSITE Clockwise from left: Gallery and sculpture at the Gillman Barracks art centre. Exterior of the Singapore Art Museum, with its statue of St John Baptist de La Salle standing with a child on either side (to commemorate the building's earlier incarnation as a school run by the La Salle brothers). It was designed by 19th-century sculptor of religious statues, Cesare Aureli. *Pedas Pedas*, a bronze chilli pepper sculpture, on the lawn behind the National Museum. It is the work of local conceptual artist, Kumari Nahappan.

A Showcase For Art

Singapore is good at reinventing itself — and its latest incarnation as South East Asia's art capital has made it put its money where its mouth is. Along with some stunning new arts' venues are such events as the Singapore Biennale, first held in 2006, and Art Stage Singapore, an annual art fair that began in 2011.

National Gallery Singapore, which cost in the region of a whopping $530 million, is the country's most significant investment, but the infrastructure also includes a high-security vault at Changi Airport where collectors can store valuable paintings and installations and an attractive development at Gillman Barracks. Here, a leafy 1930s compound that used to house British soldiers has been transformed into a venue for local and international galleries.

Similarly, St Joseph's Institution, an old Catholic boys' school, has found new life as a repository of contemporary art in the form of the Singapore Art Museum (SAM).

But, coinciding with the year that Singapore celebrated 50 years of Independence, came the opening of Singapore's jewel in its arts' crown — National Gallery Singapore. Situated in the refurbished and modified former Supreme Court and City Hall facing the Padang is a 64,000-square-metre visual art museum that houses a permanent collection built up over decades by the National Heritage Board. Its aim? To 'research, curate and present artworks with a focus on modern South East Asian and Singaporean art'. It also has a huge educational arm in the form of the Keppel Centre for Art Education, located on the ground floor of the City Hall wing.

Well Sculpted

Even though the government's Public Sculpture Masterplan was unveiled in 2003, the acquisition and display of public art has only really gained momentum in recent years. Today, Singapore's streets and parks are home to some spectacular sculptures and one even finds graffiti in designated spots along the Singapore River — a very Singaporean way of taking baby steps, when others leap!

As one *eminence grise* remarked: 'Sculptures are works of art that reflect our past, present and envisioned future.' When integrated into the cultural and physical landscape, they help shape the identity of a place — and add pleasure to any tourist itinerary.

OPPOSITE Clockwise from top left: 'First Generation' (2001), bronze, by Chong Fah Cheong, on the Singapore riverside. 60 root-like steel columns and illuminated polyhedron spheres, 'Above Below Beneath Above' (2014), by Olafur Eliasson at CapitaGreen tower. 'Singapore Soul' (2011), painted stainless steel, by Jaume Plensa at the Ocean Financial Centre. Part of 'Living World' series (2014), painted wood, by Ju Ming at CapitaGreen tower. 44-ton, 18-m high, in painted steel, 'Momentum' (2007), by David Gerstein, Finlayson Green. 'Doggy 240' (2014), painted bronze by Julien Marinetti outside ION on Orchard. 2x2 II (2014), Carrara marble, Antony Gormley, in the lobby of CapitaGreen tower. Close-up of 'La Rencontre' (2014), verdigris bronze, by Etienne, CapitaGreen tower.

Streets for People

Singapore's urban planning approach places importance in making the city people-friendly by promoting walkable, active streets and public spaces. These include boardwalks, pedestrianised streets, river walks, cycling tracks and more.

It also includes conservation, where certain buildings, streets or whole areas are gazetted and protected for their heritage value. After Singapore gained independence, the country embarked on a headlong journey to modernity that trod, to a certain extent, on existing infrastructure. Whole streets of pre-War buildings were torn down in this madcap race and it wasn't until the 1980s that the Singapore authorities began to see that there may be value in the country's architecture.

In 1989, the Urban Redevelopment Authority, the government body responsible for urban planning, launched its Conservation Masterplan whereby large swathes of Chinatown and other 'heritage areas' were gazetted as Historic Districts and Conservation Areas. As far as Chinatown is concerned, this has proved mostly beneficial. The area today is an atmospheric mix of narrow streets lined with shophouses, temples, mosques and markets. It probably doesn't look too different from when it was originally constructed to specifications drawn up in Raffles' 1822 Ordinances — even though the buildings are a lot more colourful now.

Having said that, many of Chinatown's shophouses haven't simply been preserved in aspic. With regeneration has come gentrification. Even though some shophouses retain their original purpose as shops cum living quarters, most have found new life as galleries, offices, studios, hotels, restaurants, bars and the like.

Some streets have become fully pedestrianized with shops spilling into the road, while others take on the aura of an open-air entertainment hub on specific evenings only. While some bemoan this somewhat inauthentic interpretation of history, most are content that the area's architectural treasures haven't ended up beneath a wrecker's ball — and the area may be enjoyed by Singapore's residents and tourists alike.

OPPOSITE Clockwise from top left: Colourful shutters of a conserved shophouse entice customers into a boutique. The deco facade of the old Majestic Theatre, a Cantonese opera venue, built in 1927–28 to a design by Swan & Maclaren. Decorative ceramic tiles on the exterior of shophouses first appeared around the turn of the century and add greatly to the atmosphere of the shophouse rows. ABOVE Left to right: Five-foot-way turned Parisian bistro. Guardian statue.

When one compares Singapore with other cities in South East Asia, the reality is that the former has managed to retain a significant amount of its colonial-era heritage even as it develops at breakneck speed. Wandering the streets of downtown Singapore, one stumbles across pockets of architecture frozen in time — areas where a palpable sense of history ... still remains strong.

— Kennie Ting, *The Romance of the Grand Tour*, 2015

OPPOSITE AND ABOVE The area in Chinatown between North and South Bridge Roads has been designated a car-free zone — and now sells everything from tourist tat to local foods, teas, ceramics, knick-knacks and the like. While Pagoda Street was once well-known for its opium dens, it's now the place to go for some Chinese-style retail therapy. If it's more 'made in China' than high-end, that is all part of its charm. The Chinatown Heritage Centre is also located here.

ABOVE Many of Dempsey
Hill's long airy verandahs
are lined with outdoor
seating for casual dining.
OPPOSITE From left to
right: Interior of one of
Dempsey's artisanal shops

cum restaurants. Named
after the late General Sir
Webb Gillman, a well-
known British army officer,
Gillman Barracks is now
home to a thriving art
gallery scene.

In addition to the more obvious areas of Chinatown, Kampong Glam and Little India are other pockets that have gained conservation status — and are finding new life as lifestyle hubs, artistic centres and/or food and beverage hotspots. For example, in 2012, Gillman Barracks, originally built in 1936 as a military encampment for the British Army, underwent a $10-million renovation and was transformed into a visual arts cluster. Surrounded by lush tropical greenery, it now houses a number of art galleries and positions itself as a centre for the presentation and discussion of international and South East Asian art.

Another old military encampment, the Tanglin Barracks, has become extremely popular as a foodie hangout known as Dempsey Hill. Originally British troops occupied the grounds from 1867 to 1976 — there were ten barracks buildings, each housing 50 men, wash- and cook-houses, hospital wards, a school, reading room, library and officers' quarters along with a large parade ground. Thereafter, the barracks became the Ministry of Defence (MINDEF)

headquarters, and Dempsey the place where fledgling National Servicemen reported to the military for enlistment.

Today, the barracks themselves are little changed. French red tiles have replaced the thatched attap roofs, but the long low buildings with square columns, plenty of windows and doorways providing ventilation and wrap-around verandahs remain the same. Some feature jacked roofs, double- or triple-stepped, to facilitate the expulsion of hot air — and many have wonderful greenery views.

After MINDEF left in 1989, the area gradually transformed into a quaint retail centre selling furniture, carpets and the like. Gourmet grocers, trendy boutiques, cafés and wine bars, as well as art galleries, clubs and more have now joined these early tenants. Today, the much-loved area, still surrounded by verdant jungle, is popular with locals, expatriates and tourists alike. Not too far from downtown, but still offering a rural ambience, it is a good example of architectural restoration and re-use in a fresh natural setting.

Another area that has undergone a renaissance is the first public housing estate in Singapore, known as Tiong Bahru. Comprising 20 blocks of 2- to 5-storey pre-war public housing flats built by the Singapore Improvement Trust (SIT) in the 1930s, for many years the area was a sleepy area filled with elderly residents. But once it gained conservation status in 2003, all that changed.

People saw the potential of the apartments, their style a mix of sinuous Art Moderne and Straits Style shophouse, and coveted their high ceilings, large rooms, generous balconies and terraces. It also helped that the area was so close to downtown. The result was a slew of creatives colonising an area that had previously been known mainly for its large wet market/hawker centre and Qi Tian Gong Temple, dedicated to the Monkey God.

Today Western-style coffeeshops have sent the *kopitiams* packing and quirky boutiques and independent homewares stores testify to the new residents' independent spirit. Most of the old-style grocers and hardware stores are gone, and the former Tiong Bahru Bird Arena at one end of the demolished Block 53 is no more. This was famously where men came for a coffee and a chat along with their singing birds in cages — but these days they head to the Housing Development Board flats.

Nevertheless, it isn't all doom and gloom: the straddling of old and new is something that Singapore does well, and Tiong Bahru's charm hasn't been stamped out. Aged aunties hanging out their washing on poles in the back alleys live cheek-by-jowl with the new residents and businesses — and traditional fare in the form of hawker food and local *kueh* are still some of the most sought-after in Singapore.

As one resident notes: 'Shopping and eating are the two national obsessions. Both are catered for in spectacular style in Tiong Bahru'.

OPPOSITE LEFT Facade of a SIT apartment block, originally built to help alleviate the plight of Singapore's urban poor. **OPPOSITE RIGHT A** temple dedicated to the monkey god has been present in Tiong Bahru since 1920, but this building dates from 1938.

ABOVE Clockwise from left: Quirky exterior of an independent bookstore in Tiong Bahru. Sheaf of 'joss paper', to be used as burnt offerings, in the temple. Typical *nyonya* fare at the House of Peranakan Petit, a neighbourhood restaurant run by a Peranakan family for the past 30 years.

Kampong Life

Even though there is a stereotype of the Malay as a rural soul living in a traditional Malay *kampong* or village community, in modern-day Singapore this is just that — a stereotype. However, amongst the HDB satellite towns and the urban sprawl, there remain a few vestiges of this earlier way of life. For example, on the outskirts of Bukit Brown cemetery is one old village-style mosque called Masjid Omar Salmah. Sitting on a slight elevation, it used to service the nearby Kampong Jantai that is now abandoned.

One *kampong* not abandoned, thankfully, is that of Kampong Lorong Buangkok whose Malay name is Selak Kain meaning 'to hitch up one's sarong'; this comes from the practice of people raising their sarongs to wade through water during flash floods.

Hemmed in by encroaching high-rises, Lorong Buangkok seems a million miles away from the rest of Singapore. Covering an area of about three football fields, it contains a cluster of *kampong*-style zinc-roofed houses containing around 30 families, 18 or which are Chinese and 10 Malay. There is a *sarau* or prayer room, and village matters are presided over by a headman. All around are the fruits, vegetables and flowers traditionally grown in Malay villages — jackfruit, banana, tomatoes, lime, for example, as well as hibiscus, morning glory and butterfly pea flowers.

The land was bought by a Traditional Chinese Medicine practitioner in 1956 — and is now rented out by his daughter to the various households for a minimal sum. The Urban Redevelopment Authority has indicated that the *kampong* may not be saved from the march of progress and redevelopment is almost inevitable. As such, Kampong Lorong Buangkok is certainly worth a visit now, before it's too late.

LEFT Built in traditional style, this mosque was constructed in 1973–1974, with support from Syed Ibrahim bin Omar Alsagoff, a member of the Alsagoff family. It was named after Syed Ibrahim's parents, Syed Omar and Salmah. OPPOSITE Four views of picturesque Kampong Lorong Buangkok.

Kopi Old

Kopi is the Malay/Hokkien term for coffee and refers to the 'old-style' coffee served in a *kopitiam* or traditional coffee shop. Originally furnished with marble-topped tables and bent-wood chairs, but now more likely to sport plastic, such venues offer a variety of foods based on egg, toast and *kaya* (coconut jam), plus coffee, tea and Milo, a malted chocolate drink popular in South East Asia.

LEFT Condensed milk is added to *kopi* and served with *kaya* toast.
RIGHT Octogenarian Mr Shi makes coffee the traditional way in his Heap Seng Leong coffeeshop where time seems to have been momentarily halted. Different styles of *kopitiam*.

Coffee New

Unsurprisingly in a country that loves its coffee, all the big brands are now ubiquitous over the island. However, there are also a number of marvellous independent micro coffee roasters that are making waves in unlikely HDB or downtown locations. Singaporeans drink a lot of coffee, so it's hardly surprising that this authentic caffeine scene is thriving.

LEFT Home-roasted and brewed coffee at specialty coffee shop NYLON.
RIGHT Dean and Deluca interior, transported from NYC to Orchard. Ann Siang shophouse style. NYLON has standing room only. Cool vibe at COO.

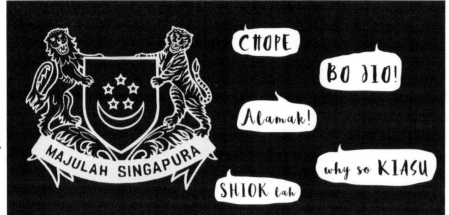

Essential Singapore

Some things are quintessentially Singaporean, and simply are not found anywhere else on the planet. If you live here, they're part and parcel of everyday life. For visitors they can be a source of bemusement. Check them out for size, clockwise from above:

Singapore Colloquial English or Singlish is a cornerstone of the nation's culture. Colourful and snappy, it incorporates other languages into the national language of English — and generally results in shorter, ungrammatical sentences or phrases that have a wonderful character and lilt.

A Hokkien and Singlish word that translates as 'a grasping, selfish attitude' or 'fear of failure', *kiasu* refers to a type of anxious, selfish behaviour that is characterized by a fear of losing out. It is generally seen as a negative trait, used to refer to someone who thinks of themselves first and acts in an over-competitive manner.

For all manner of takeaway drinks — from juices, to coffee or *teh tarik* — you are likely to be given a to-go bag rather than a disposable cup. The plastic bag, tied with a lanyard and stuffed with a straw, is a familiar sight on Singapore's streets.

Regarded by many South East Asian peoples as the 'king of fruits', the durian has a distinctive odour that has been variously described as rotten, repugnant and similar to sewage. Because the smell tends to linger, it has been banned from public transport and public buildings in many Asian countries. Nevertheless, many people are avid fans of the taste — and demand is high during durian season.

Considered one of the national dishes of Singapore, chicken rice is adapted from an early recipe brought by Chinese immigrants originally from Hainan. Poached chicken is served with chicken broth, 'oily rice' or rice cooked in stock with ginger, garlic and pandan leaves, and cucumber.

First created in 1915 at Raffles Hotel by bartender Ngiam Tong Boon, the Singapore Sling is widely regarded as the national drink of the country. A gin-based cocktail, it also contains pineapple juice, grenadine, lime juice and Dom Benedictine. Slightly sickly, very sweet.

Buying a house? Driving to dinner? Paying your taxes? You'll be leaving your HDB, taking the PIE, and heading to IRAS. Efficient, yet expressive, Singapore's acronyms are part of the nation's culture.

Half-lion, half-fish and fully ridiculous, the merlion is a creature that was originally devised as a logo for the Singapore Tourist Board, and has now become the national symbol of the country. Multiple statues, including a huge 37-m edifice on Sentosa, are dotted around the island.

OPPOSITE Characterful Singlish expressions and the lilting tone of Singlish are part of the nation's unique character. If you *chope* you are making a reservation; if something's *shiok*, it is cool; *alamak*, originally Portuguese, expresses shock or surprise. This little book, *An Essential Guide to Singlish* (Gartbooks) is a local bestseller with over 100,000 copies sold. ABOVE Clockwise from top left: Coffee in plastic bag; durian; Hainanese chicken rice; Singapore Sling at Raffles; road sign for the Tampines, Seletar and Central expressways; merlion at the mouth of the Singapore River.

> *"People admire the incredible progress that Singapore has made in creating prosperity and opportunity for its people and for being an excellent international partner.... I think we've seen that although Singapore does not have a large population, it punches above its weight, because of its wise policies, and ability to work with all countries."*
>
> — Barack Obama, 2015

Homegrown Talent

Within Singapore, fashion houses like Club 21, Raoul and Charles & Keith are well known, while department stores like Tangs and Robinsons are old favourites. Similarly, Tung Lok and Crystal Jade are well regarded food companies and most people bank with local banks: UOB (United Overseas Bank), DBS (Development Bank of Singapore) and the like.

Global brands, however, are few — hardly surprising when one considers that Singapore only has a population of around 5.75 million people. Nonetheless, there are some Singaporean companies and brands that have gained international recognition. We showcase them here.

OPPOSITE Clockwise from top left: The country's flag carrier, Singapore Airlines, currently ranked third in global rankings, is nonetheless the most awarded airline in the world. Gourmet beverage firm, launched in Singapore in 2007 as a subsidiary of The Wellness Group (TWG), has been phenomenally successful with its slew of high-end teas and tea paraphernalia. Banyan Tree Holdings is an international hospitality brand that manages and develops resorts, hotels and spas in Asia, America, Africa and the Middle East.

It was established in 1994, with its roots in Singapore. Founded by Singaporean entrepreneur, Christina Ong, the COMO Group comprises fashion group Club 21, COMO Hotels and Resorts and wellness brand COMO Shambhala. COMO Hotels are found in locations from Asia to London to the Caribbean and are renowned for their design cachet, sustainability principles and for crafting unique experiences. Fraser and Neave was set up by John Fraser and David Neave more than a century ago, when they diversified from their original printing

business to pioneer the aerated water and soft drinks business in South East Asia in 1883. Sold in almost 50 countries, Axe Brand Universal Oil had its beginnings in a little shophouse in South Bridge Road 85 years ago. The clear medicated oil is, today, a household name. It may not be known worldwide yet, but it certainly deserves to be: Wild Rice is a professional theatre company started in 2000 by talented actor, playwright and director Ivan Heng. Over nearly two decades it has become a much-loved player on the local stage.

Iconic Buildings

Judges at the eighth annual World Architecture Festival (WAF) awarded the top prize to a housing development in Singapore known as The Interlace. This is only one of the prizes that Singapore has won. Despite its size, the country is recognized as a global player on the world's architectural stage.

Architect, professor and author Robert Powell notes in his book *Singapore Good Class Bungalow 1819–2015* that 'it is a thought-provoking comment on the new world order that in 2012, 2013, 2014 and 2015 the World Architecture Festival — the largest celebration of new and emerging architecture in the world — was held in Singapore and it was to Singapore that architects from around the world came for enlightenment'.

Yes and no. Certainly the country punches far above its weight when one considers population size versus output, but when one looks back in history one sees a prodigious amount of architectural talent. From early colonial structures through modernism to the present day, the city boasts an extraordinary variety of styles in both the public and private sector. With space constraints, we are able to showcase only a handful here.

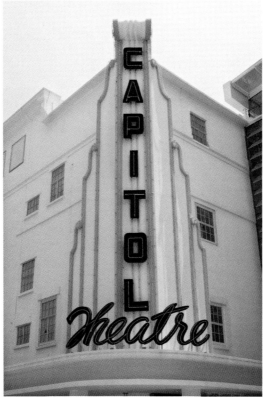

OPPOSITE AND ABOVE
Clockwise from left:
Private condominium,
Reflections at Keppel Bay,
Daniel Libeskind, 2013. Six
glass towers at alternating
heights of between 24 and
41 storeys rise like beacons
of light at the water's edge.
The Pinnacle@Duxton, an
award-winning 50-storey HDB
residential development,
ARC Studio Architecture
+ Urbanism, with RSP
Architects Planners &
Engineers, 2013. Raffles
Hotel, designed by Regent
Alfred John Bidwell of
Swan & Maclaren and built
on the site of the original
Beach House. 1899. Marina
Bay Sands (MBS), Moshe
Safdie and Associates,
2010. Expressionist corner
shophouse as wannabe
tower, Ho Kwong Yew,
1938. Capitol Theatre, Keys
& Dowdeswell, 1938, in Art
Deco style. Former Kallang
Airport, designed by Frank
Dorrington Ward, in early
modernist style with Art
Deco interiors. 1938.

THIS WAS SINGAPORE

"Singapore city has come a long way: it is an example of what can be achieved when there is political will to set goals and to achieve these ... it has the potential to present itself as a textbook example of a good sustainable city environment."

— Ole Johan Dale, *Urban Planning in Singapore*, 1999

Singapore in the 1960s

The turbulent decade of the 1960s, Singapore's first years as an independent nation, was a pivotal one in the country's history. As this selection of postcards testifies, Singapore was already a well-established city with a thriving port, a handsome built environment with strong infrastructure, and a vibrant cultural life. What it lacked was a common post-colonial identity.

This the government sought to build in those early years. As Henry Kissinger noted in his obituary to Lee Kuan Yew in 2015, 'He asserted that a city located on a sandbar with nary an economic resource to draw upon, and whose major industry as a colonial naval base had disappeared, could nevertheless thrive and achieve international stature by building on its principal asset: the intelligence, industry and dedication of its people'.

This is what this book has sought to showcase. Ending with a chapter on how, when and where Independence started allows us to reflect on the past. These glorious images essentially tell the same story: then as now, Singapore stands at the crossroads of East and West; it's just that now it exists in a more globalized world.

PREVIOUS PAGE
Mid 20th-century view
of Chinatown with stalls
spilling out from the five-
foot-way into the street.
OPPOSITE The 1869
Cavenagh Bridge. *Tongkangs*
and barges ply between
godowns on the river's
bank and ships anchored
in the harbour.

ABOVE Clockwise from
top left: Battery Road,
with the Bank of China in
the centre. A panoramic
view of Raffles Quay with
Clifford Pier. Clifford Pier
and Change Alley, with
ships in the harbour. The
International Airport of
Singapore, in the 1960s
located at Paya Lebar.

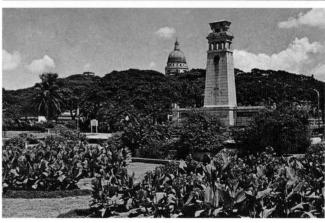

OPPOSITE TOP Aerial view of the city with Beach Road stretching out to the east coast.
OPPOSITE BELOW Raffles Place, bordered by bank buildings and department stores.
ABOVE Clockwise from top left: Railway station and Railway Hotel at Tanjong Pagar. Collyer Quay. British Military Hospital, Alexandra Road. The Cenotaph, Queen Elisabeth Walk, Esplanade. Lim Bo Seng Memorial, Queen Elisabeth Walk, Esplanade. Former National Theatre, built in 1963 and demolished in 1986.

ABOVE Typical street
scene in Chinatown with
stalls selling paraphernalia
for the annual Chinese
New Year festival.

ABOVE Clockwise from top left: Singapore Botanic Gardens, Cluny Road. Indian snake charmers at Mount Faber. Chinese Chamber of Commerce, Hill Street. Happy World Amusement Park, one of three such entertainment centres in Singapore. It closed in 2000. Gateway to Haw Par Villa, Pasir Panjang. Aerial view of Singapore Harbour.

OPPOSITE TOP Sultan Mosque, the centre for Singapore's Muslims, North Bridge Road.
OPPOSITE BELOW Sri Mariamman Temple, South Bridge Road, Singapore's oldest Hindu temple.
ABOVE Clockwise from top left: Houses on stilts on an island opposite Singapore Harbour. A pig farm and *kampong* life in rural Singapore. Typical downtown barber's shop. Busy thoroughfare of North Bridge Road. Hong Lim Park, with semi-circular auditorium. Trishaw and driver awaiting a customer.

CREDITS

All photos taken by Jacob Termansen with the exception of p23 (the Padang), p66 (lithograph of Singapore River) and pp118–119 (Chinatown), courtesy of the estate of Luca Invernizzi Tettoni; Map of Singapore (p32), courtesy of the Royal Geographical Society, London; View of Singapore from Government Hill (pp52–53) and View of Singapore from the Harbour (p54), courtesy of a private collector; Singapore Theatre Festival 2016 poster, courtesy of Wild Rice (P114); all 1960s postcards (pp120–127) courtesy of Hsien Yoong How, except for the Happy World postcard courtesy of Lim Kheng Chye (p125).

Further thanks to the following for allowing us to photograph on their premises: Thian Hock Keng Temple; (pp56–7); The Chinatown Heritage Centre (pp60–61); the Peranakan Museum (pp60–61); The Eurasian Association (p76); the Chesed-el Synagogue (pp78–79); COO Hostel (p96 and p113); National Gallery Singapore (p98); Qi Tian Gong Temple (pp108–9); Kampong Lorong Buangkok (p111); Keap Seng Leong coffeeshop (p112); NYLON specialty coffee roasters (pp112–113); Raffles Hotel (pp115, 119).

Thanks to the following for allowing reproduction of quotes:
The late Lee Kuan Yew; Lee Hsien Loong; Moshe Safdie; https://www.ura.gov.sg/; https://www.sbg.org.sg/; https://www.nparks.gov.sg/; Sinnathamby Rajaratnam; https://www.designsingapore.org/; https://www.nac.gov.sg/; Mah Bow Tan; the late Benjamin Cook; Barack Obama; Henry Kissinger.

Further excerpts taken from:
Memoir of the life and public services of Sir Thomas Stamford Raffles, F.R.S., &c. &c., particularly in the government of Java, 1811–1816, Bencoolen and its dependencies, 1817–1824, Raffles, Sophia Lady, 1835; *Black and White, the Singapore House 1898–1941,* Julian Davison, 2014; *Memories of Chinatown,* Geraldene Lowe-Ismail, 2016; *The Golden Chersonese and the Way Thither,* Isabella Bird, 1883; *Singapore Shophouse,* Julian Davison, 2010; *A History of Modern Singapore 1819–2005,* C M Turnbull, 2009; 'Tribute to Heroes', LTC Andy Tan, 2005; *The Romance of the Grand Tour,* Kennie Ting, 2015; *An Essential Guide to Singlish,* Gartbooks, 2003; *Urban Planning in Singapore,* Ole Johan Dale, 1999.

ACKNOWLEDGMENTS

The publisher, author and photographer would like to thank the following for their help during the production of this book:

Edwin Low and Priscilla Potts of Supermama/Kihara Inc; PARKROYAL on Pickering; Map Collections at the Royal Geographical Society, London; Chinatown Heritage Centre; Kennie Ting from the Peranakan Museum and the Asian Civilisations Museum; the Baba House; Lester Lowe and Edward DaSilva of the Eurasian Association; Rebecca Rott; Ronni Pinsler; Solomon Solomon and the Chesed-el Synagogue; Fort Siloso museum; Memories at Old Ford Factory museum; Reflections at Bukit Chandu interpretive centre; Changi Museum and Chapel; Kranji War Memorial; Joyce Seah at Ministry of Design; the owners of COO hostel; Gillman Barracks; Thian Hock Keng Temple; Qi Tian Gong Temple; the residents at Kampong Lorong Buangkok; Mr Shi at Keap Seng Leong coffeeshop; Raffles Hotel; Dean and Deluca; NYLON specialty coffee roasters; William Gartshore; Singapore Airlines; The Wellness Group (TWG); Banyan Tree Holdings; COMO Group; Fraser & Neave; Tiger beer; AXE Brand; Wild Rice; Hsien Yoong How; Lim Kheng Chye; Paul Haines.